SCOTLAND'S WESTERN SEABOARD

BY

G. DOUGLAS BOLTON

WITH EIGHTY-FOUR
PHOTOGRAPHS BY
THE AUTHOR

OLIVER AND BOYD
EDINBURGH: TWEEDDALE COURT
LONDON: GREAT RUSSELL STREET, W.C.

FIRST PUBLISHED . . . 1953

PRINTED IN GREAT BRITAIN BY
ROBERT CUNNINGHAM AND SONS LTD., ALVA
FOR OLIVER AND BOYD LTD., EDINBURGH

ACKNOWLEDGMENTS

My grateful thanks are due to the following:

The Editor of *Scotland's Magazine* for kind permission to reproduce extracts from my two articles on Knapdale and the Kinlochbervie district which first appeared in that journal.

The Editor of *The Autocar* for kind permission to reproduce extracts from my article on the Cape Wrath district first printed in that journal.

The Editor of *Out of Doors and Countrygoer* for kind permission to reproduce extracts from my article on the Isle of Skye first published in that journal.

Miss Vivienne Knight, formerly of Vega Productions Ltd., for kind permission to quote from information on the subject of the Corrievreckan sequences of the Michael Powell and Emeric Pressburger production *I Know Where I'm Going*.

Mr Ian S. Mackenzie, proprietor of the Crinan Hotel, and Messrs David MacBrayne Ltd. for much valuable information about the Whirlpool of Corrievreckan.

Mr Donald McLeod of Kinlochbervie for authentic information on the subject of the late Sandy Gunn's encounter with a mermaid at Sandwood Bay near Cape Wrath.

G. DOUGLAS BOLTON

'LOCHALINE'
BROMLEY ROAD
SHIPLEY, YORKS

CONTENTS

CONTENTS

MAP .. P. 111
       "   P. 3
       "   P. 47

LIST OF ILLUSTRATIONS

LIST OF ILLUSTRATIONS

LIST OF ILLUSTRATIONS

INTRODUCTION

THIS is not a guide book, nor is it a book for the mountaineer or long distance walker who likes to leave the beaten track. It is essentially a book for the discriminating tourist—preferably with a car at his disposal.

In selecting Scotland's western seaboard I have chosen perhaps the most picturesque, colourful and fascinating area in Britain, and this book is the record of many years of personal visits. Although well-known places of tourist interest have not been overlooked, I have tried to emphasise the merits of lesser known and more remote places by describing my own visits. Many such places are approached by indifferent roads, but none are beyond the reach of the owner of a modern car.

The book is divided into chapters, each of which could form the basis for a separate tour, and as the interest increases the further north we go, it is better to start from the south. Although our journey really begins at the Mull of Galloway, the most south-westerly point of Scotland, the logical approach is from the Solway and along the Galloway coast, thus including the southern seaboard.

Historical references are kept to a minimum, and are only included to encourage an interest in the past rather than to satisfy it. In describing personal experiences I have tried to keep a proper balance between the places described and give to each one its due.

What is the best method of touring Scotland, and in particular its western seaboard? In short, where, when and how to go? These questions in turn involve others such as the time at our disposal, the weather, accommodation and modes of transport.

Let us first consider transport. It is quite possible to tour Scotland on foot, but we must not pretend that every yard of the tour is full of interest. It is often necessary to traverse dull, flat and busy main roads in order to reach places of interest, and the walker would have to sacrifice whole days in this way—days which would be better spent in a more leisurely survey of the more interesting places. In this respect the cyclist is much better off, for he can cover greater distances.

The motorist has every advantage because he can travel with the minimum of effort and use his car as a base for expeditions on foot. But a car must be used with intelligence. It is a waste of time and petrol to keep to the main roads and rush about the country without purpose or objective.

The vast wealth of tourist interest is not confined to the roadside. The motorist must occasionally use his feet and be prepared to walk a mile or two if necessary to reach some notable scene.

The purpose of this book is to arouse your interest in many worth-while places and perhaps give you the inclination to visit some of them yourself. Each chapter forms a separate whole, although all are arranged in sequence. Chapters can be aggregated to cover quite lengthy tours. Although the subject matter is the western seaboard, inland places are mentioned within easy reach of the coast. But aimless wandering will give little satisfaction. Some people like to set out on a touring holiday without any set plan. They may by chance come across a few of the castles, abbeys and beauty spots with which Scotland abounds, but they could have done so very much better with a preliminary itinerary.

It may be argued that the western seaboard is best seen from the sea. I think it a disadvantage to see everything from sea-level, and except for occasional landing places the coast itself is beyond reach. You are separated continually from cliff and beach by a wide stretch of water. The approach from land may be much harder, but the roads do climb and wind around the very scenes which you wish to enjoy. You can wander down to the beach or enjoy wonderful landscapes and colourful sunsets from the viewpoints of some high road pass. You can meet the people, visit the castles and make contact with the beauty spots. But there is no reason why you should not add diversion to your wayfaring by occasional sea-trips. With the exception of Skye, the Inner and Outer Hebrides can only be visited by steamer or by certain air routes. The attraction of the western seaboard is bound up with the many glimpses of the Inner Hebrides, and I have included accounts of

2

2 Castle Kennedy
and White Loch,
Wigtownshire

COUNTIES OF WIGTOWN AND DUMFRIES

The flooded Nith
Dumfries

3

brief visits to some of the more attractive isles. I have not touched the Outer Hebrides, as they merit a book to themselves.

Supposing you have no car, and motor coach, cycling and walking holidays do not appeal, there is much to be said for careful selection of a centre for local excursions, such as Oban, Fort William or Dunoon.

The best weather is undoubtedly in May, and it is in May that you stand the best chance of accommodation without previous booking. At times you may get wild weather, often more impressive than any summer day of heat haze and cloudless skies. But rarely will there be any long spell of bad weather in May. You are more likely to get long spells of sunshine with picture clouds in the sky and all the freshness of springtime. Next to May, your best chance of settled weather will be in June or September, but chance accommodation will be a problem even if you travel alone. But in September the problem decreases as the month advances, and if you avoid the more popular places you should encounter little difficulty. July and August are the doubtful months for weather; moreover, unless accommodation has been booked in advance, there will be little hope of a vacant room.

There are many types of accommodation, and it is a great mistake to think that good hotels are necessarily expensive. Scottish hotels are mostly very good indeed, and a kindly welcome is the rule rather than the exception. The Automobile Association Members Handbook and the Royal Automobile Club Guide and Handbook give full details of their respective appointed hotels, and the Scottish Tourist Board's 'Where to Stay in Scotland' gives exhaustive information about almost all available accommodation in the whole of Scotland, ranging from inexpensive lodgings to the most palatial hotels.

My own methods of touring may prove of interest. Being a professional photographer specialising in British scenery I have to make many lengthy photographic tours, hence it is vital to make the best use of my time. I have found the following system ideal for touring—and it would be just as suitable for a holiday.

The itinerary is prepared with great care. The route is roughly prepared, and then details are added after a careful analysis of the potentialities of each place and district. A set of routes is then listed to include all the places and scenes of special interest to be visited. I then decide how long the entire trip will take, given fine weather. I allow a few days in excess of this, and set forth—generally each May and September. If the weather is fine I know where to finish each night, and can thus book accommodation a few hours in advance. If the weather is hopeless I use my spare days by waiting for better conditions. In doubtful weather I go on, because a doubtful morning in the Highlands generally means a fine afternoon and evening. In this way I can carry on to the end of my allotted time, my itinerary being delayed or advanced according to the weather. Such a plan would also make the best use of *your* time.

Finally, whatever else you forget, remember to take a set of good maps. You will need them.

CHAPTER ONE

CARLISLE TO PORTPATRICK

THE road from Carlisle to Gretna is a fast one, and seems to urge one to hurry over the border. But halt a while at Metalbridge for your first glimpse of the Solway. Although there may be little magic in the scene, it is the beginning of our long and fascinating journey round Scotland's western seaboard. On that account the view takes on a new importance, and if you should arrive at sunset the flat Solway shores will be a blaze of light, and a subtle, intangible feeling of excitement will beckon you onwards.

After traversing that queer no-man's-land between the Esk and the Sark, the border is crossed at Sark Bridge, and here you will see Scotland's First House, or Ye Old Toll Bar. Over 10,000 marriages have been performed in this celebrated whitewashed cottage.

Gretna Green is a little village a mile to the north, and the old Blacksmith's Shop is a positive Mecca for tourists. This is another whitewashed single-storey building which bears a number of conspicuous notices inviting you inside. The Gretna Green legend suggests a romantic entry into Scotland, but the surrounding country does little more than hint at the more satisfying scenery later to be encountered.

A long speedway continues through low-lying country to Annan, and distances are soon covered. Annan is a royal burgh and a typical Lowland town. Robert the Bruce once had a castle on the site of the present Town Hall. Cross the substantial bridge over the River Annan, and descend to a pleasant walk beside the river bank. There is a fine view of the town from just beyond the weir. When the river is low there are banks of pebbles where children can generally be found throwing stones into the water—a rather catching diversion which often extends into middle age.

Beyond Annan there are two routes to Dumfries. The Cummertrees road is nearer to the coast, but the Carrutherstown route is at a greater elevation and gives better views of the Solway. On the other hand there is a very fine Runic Cross in Cummertrees Church—so you must take your choice. On clear days there are extensive views westwards to Criffell on the Galloway coast and southwards across the Solway to the Cumberland mountains.

Do not be misled by the rather uninviting approach to Dumfries. It is a town steeped in the tradition of 'Rabbie' Burns and it takes time to appreciate its attractions. You will be more impressed when you have followed one of the narrow alleys leading from the High Street to the River Nith.

The road by the river expands into a vast open space, and there are benches on the riverside walk where you can sit in peace. The Nith falls in a series of bustling cascades just below an ancient and picturesque bridge built in 1280 by Devorgilla. I remember listening to a pipe band and watching the pastel tints of a tropical sunset beyond the silhouetted roof-line of old Dumfries. A number of local children were swimming and splashing about in the river, and balancing precariously on the edges of the waterfalls. Oblivious of it all a fisherman stood in eternal hope. It only needed 'Rabbie' Burns to emerge from the past and invite me to the Old Globe Tavern.

There are popular walks by the side of the Nith both to the north and south of the town, and a favourite drive is to follow the river southwards to its estuary into the Solway. The road joins the estuary at Kelton, and from there to Glencaple runs alongside a grey expanse of mudbanks. The attractive village of Glencaple faces the estuary and looks westwards across the mudbanks to the dominating contours of Criffell. This is a place of wonderful sunsets, and even the mud reflects rainbow tints. The scene is very different at high water, but to my mind there is a curious and rather sinister attraction about a broad estuary at low water. It is as if a new and rather unpleasant world is exposed, but one made beautiful by reflected light and the strange patterns of the mudbanks.

The road continues to Bowhouse and meanders placidly alongside the ever-widening estuary to the broad expanse of the Solway. Just beyond Bowhouse a footpath leads to Caerlaverock Castle, a moated ruin of striking appearance. Much of the castle still remains, and the walls are surmounted by a machicolated cornice. The castle is somewhat triangular in shape with an impressive gatehouse at the apex and a round tower at each corner. The

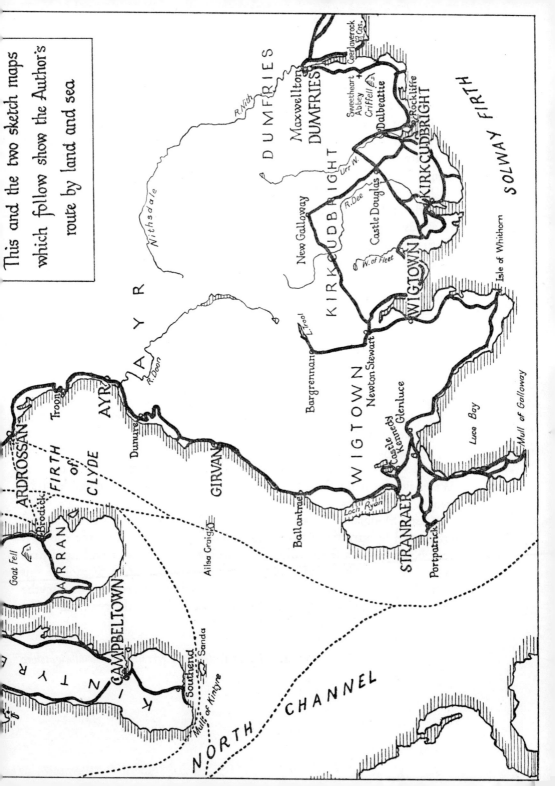

This and the two sketch maps which follow show the Author's route by land and sea

steep walls rising from the moat contribute to the rather forbidding appearance of this great stronghold.

Do not miss Lincluden Abbey to the north of Dumfries near the banks of the Nith. Burns was a frequent visitor here, and the fine red sandstone ruins are still worth a visit. More Burns associations at Dumfries may be seen at Burns House and the Burns Mausoleum.

New Abbey is a colourful village near the slopes of Criffell, but its main attraction is Sweetheart Abbey—as romantic as its name. This red sandstone ruin was founded by Devorgilla, who married John Balliol. After his death she had his heart embalmed and kept it in a casket, which was with her to the end of her days. When she died, the heart was interred with her at Sweetheart Abbey. Devorgilla had much to her credit; it was she who endowed Balliol College at Oxford, formerly founded by her husband.

At Kirkbean you can follow a narrow road southwards to the coast village of Southerness (Satterness) if you wish to see a queer lighthouse, now disused; all around are vast open spaces and innumerable rock-pools.

A winding road leads to Rockcliffe, one of the most picturesque resorts in Galloway, and directly opposite Rough Island. At high tide the water creeps up to the margin of the road and makes a colourful foreground to the distant Galloway hills. The scene is overlooked by cosy houses which nestle by the wayside.

The Mote of Urr is an Anglo-Norman earthwork, and one of the best examples in Scotland. It is prominently situated on a hillock near the Urr Water not far from Dalbeattie, is circular in shape, and is surrounded by a trench.

Castle Douglas is one of my favourite Galloway towns. It is clean and bright and in attractive surroundings. Carlingwark Loch, to the south, is very beautiful on a fresh, colourful morning, and here you will find small boys fishing, rowing, and exploring the islets which are a feature of this loch; or perhaps you will see a solitary roadman sharpening his scythe preparatory to cutting the verge between the loch and the road. In places

Plate 4. Golden waters at Creetown, Kirkcudbrightshire

the trees form an arch across the road; elsewhere there is an uninterrupted view across the blue waters of the loch to distant grey hills. There is a fine walk to Threave Castle, on an island on the River Dee, a short distance to the west. This grim ruin has gloomy memories emphasised by a 'hanging stone' over the doorway.

The coast road to Auchencairn passes near Palnackie, where you will be surprised to find a small harbour on the Urr Water. It is worth another digression to Orchardton to see the famous Round Tower, dating from the twelfth century. This curious tower is forty feet high with walls six feet thick, surmounted by a small cap-house.

The best view of Dundrennan Abbey is gained from the top of the wall to the north. From here the grey ruins, enhanced by the grace of the pointed arches and the restful green of the closely cropped grass, form a quiet harmony in which there is not one dissentient note. This ancient abbey was built in 1142 for Cistercian monks from distant Rievaulx in Yorkshire. It was here, on 15th May 1568, that Mary Queen of Scots passed her last night on Scottish soil before sailing across the Solway to England from a lonely stretch of the shore now called Port Mary.

I remember approaching this lovely corner of the Kirkcudbright coast from Abbey Burnfoot. There was no sound beyond the surf as it fell on the pebbly beach. The beach must shelve steeply, as the waves approached in the form of glass-like undulations to within a short distance of where I stood, and then broke with an unassuming grace beautiful to watch. This is a lovely corner of Galloway, and I was again captivated on the approach to Kirkcudbright where the road creeps down to the sea opposite St. Mary's Isle, a small peninsula where you will come across the ruins of a priory.

There is a leisurely spaciousness about Kirkcudbright. Its wide streets, tree-shaded nooks, ancient castle and tolbooth, with the picturesque white-washed houses near the harbour, form a pleasant scene, reminiscent of bygone days. The broad, muddy waters of the River Dee are spanned by a modern but not undignified bridge. The harbour is a haven for small craft,

Plate 5. Water of Minnock near Glen Trool, Kirkcudbrightshire

5

but little else, for the shallow estuary becomes a sea of glistening mud at low water. Little remains of the castle, whose grim outline is a conspicuous landmark. Whitewashed buildings rise abruptly from the mud, and various small craft lie sprawling in various positions, awaiting the tide. Kirkcudbright is much favoured by artists, and on my many visits through the years I have always found something new to photograph—a familiar scene given new life by changed weather conditions.

Kirkcudbright is a royal burgh and the ancient seat of the Stewartry. You should stay a while to become acquainted with its wistful charm. Although it is not a large town it has a character all its own.

A picturesque road leads to Tongland and Bridge of Dee to the north-east. The road south to Borgue keeps alongside the estuary, and there is also a direct road to Gatehouse-of-Fleet. This is a quiet, unassuming town with the imposing Cally Palace Hotel situated in extensive grounds surrounding a lake. An attempt was once made to turn the River Fleet into a canal, and to open factories and a shipyard at Gatehouse, but the venture was not a success. The coast road from Gatehouse to Creetown along the shores of Wigtown Bay is one of the most delightful routes in Galloway. The view from the riverside looking back to Gatehouse is a mixture of river and pasture, trees and distant moorland. The ruins of Cardoness Castle crown a hillock nearby, and although little more than the tall and forbidding keep remains, this fifteenth century stronghold is worth seeing.

There are embracing views of the blue waters of Wigtown Bay all the way to Creetown, and despite its proximity to the shore the road is well wooded. Many gaps between the trees give frequent glimpses of golden sands and richly coloured rocks. The scene is at its best at high water, and, is particularly fine on a clear, sparkling, sunny day with brilliant clouds. Several well-shaped and conveniently placed rocks make excellent seats, and perhaps you will find time to spend a lazy afternoon here and enjoy the scene at leisure. There are a number of caves on this rock-bound coast, the best known being Dirk Hatteraick's Cave just beyond Ravenshall Point. The remains of Carsluith Castle are passed on the approach to Creetown. The trees give way to extensive views across the seaweed-strewn shore to the gentle contours of distant Galloway hills, but only a clear sunny day can

6

show the scene to advantage. Beyond Creetown the fast main road follows the Cree estuary to Newton Stewart.

Newton Stewart is an excellent touring centre. The best views of the town are from the substantial and graceful stone bridge which spans the Cree on the approach from the east. Just below the bridge the river falls in an impressive cascade over a weir, and there is a grand view to the north. The river is broad and stately, and the grey houses rise in bewildering array from the waterside.

One of the finest routes from Newton Stewart is the moorland road to New Galloway, passing Murray's monument and Clatteringshaws reservoir. There are distant views of the Rhinns of Kells and the Merrick, the most mountainous and desolate region in the whole of southern Scotland, best approached from the head of Loch Trool. Glen Trool and Loch Trool are the scenic gems of the south-west. The loch is cradled beneath impressive hills dominated by the Merrick, and the scene is almost Highland in character. A passable road leads to the head of the loch, but beyond that the forbidding territory around Loch Enoch and the Merrick is only approached on foot.

The Machers is a broad and rather dull peninsula extending many miles to the south from Newton Stewart. At Burrow Head it is nearly as far south as the Mull of Galloway. Wigtown is another royal burgh perched on a hill, and has an air of belonging to the past—and a not too cheerful past at that! There is a wide open space in the centre of the town around which the houses gaze sleepily. The harbour at the mouth of the River Bladnoch is disused. The story of the Wigtown Martyrs—whose graves are in the churchyard—takes us back to the days of the Covenanters. In 1685 a woman of 63 and a girl of 18 were tied to stakes at low water near the mouth of the river and left to drown by the rising tide.

Whithorn, birthplace of St. Ninian, has as its principal features of interest the twelfth century priory and the recently discovered Candida Casa. St. Ninian may be said to have introduced Christianity into Scotland long before St. Columba landed at Iona, and still longer before St. Augustine came to England in 597. This leap into the past takes us back to the last days of Roman Britain, when Magnus Maximus had the bitter task of withdrawing the garrisons from Hadrian's Wall in 383. St. Ninian was a

Romanised Briton, and was allowed to travel without hindrance. During his wanderings in Europe he became greatly influenced by St. Martin of Tours. He returned to Whithorn in 397, and began to build his little white church, the Candida Casa of history, on a site which was long a matter of conjecture. During my last visit to Whithorn in 1949 excavations were being made in the grounds of the Priory Church, with the result that Candida Casa saw the light of day once more, probably one of the most dramatic discoveries of its kind ever to be made. Today at Whithorn you can see a tangible link with the St. Ninian of 1556 years ago.

Other links with St. Ninian take us across the rather dull territory of the Machers to the remote fishing village of Isle of Whithorn, a quiet haven which will come as a great surprise after traversing so much uninspiring scenery.

What is the spell of Isle of Whithorn? I think its quality is due to a sleepy remoteness and the picturesque appearance of its whitewashed cottages. Walk to the harbour and along to the end of the quay. The houses give the odd impression of being anchored to the mud, as if only awaiting high water to sail away.

The ruins of the nearby St. Ninian's Chapel have no connexion with the saint, the present remains dating only from the thirteenth century, but it is fairly certain that he did settle here for a time, possibly on this very site.

Some two miles to the west of Burrow Head, approached from Physgill, is St. Ninian's Cave, where no doubt he came to meditate. Early Christian crosses found here can be seen in the museum at Whithorn Priory, but crosses still remain incised on the walls of the cave and on the rocks outside.

Even today it is rough work wandering around this wild Galloway coast, but it must have been immeasurably worse in the early fifth century.

Perhaps the best view of Isle of Whithorn, which is not an island but a peninsula, can be seen from the west on the approach from Whithorn. The harbour then seems very spacious and the village gives an impression of size and importance which a closer inspection dispels. No doubt the atmosphere of drowsy languor may disappear in bad weather, but on a hot day one creeps about as silently as a cat in order not to disturb the all-pervading hush.

Some roads are only attractive on account of the distant views they offer, and are apt to prove disappointing in hazy weather. The road from Isle of Whithorn to Glenluce along the shores of Luce Bay falls into this category. Whenever I have followed this route it has been intensely hot and hazy, with the result that all colour seemed to have been drained away by the heat. Under such conditions all that can be said is that the road is dull and dreary to Port William, a small holiday resort which might be attractive under better conditions. From Port William to Glenluce much of the road keeps very close to a rather monotonous shore. Despite a rocky beach there are no cliffs of any size.

Do not be misled by the rather dull drive from Glenluce to Portpatrick, where we make our first contact with the west coast. The somewhat uninteresting approach increases our pleasure on arrival.

CHAPTER TWO

PORTPATRICK TO GREENOCK

PORTPATRICK is a place of sharp contrasts. It is built around a fine harbour, constructed a century ago to develop trade with Ireland, but owing to the severity of the winter gales Stranraer has now superseded Portpatrick as a port. Hence the harbour seems rather battered and forlorn today. The houses, too, around the harbour and the main street, take on a careworn appearance in contrast to the more modern and prosperous upper level of the town, dominated by the huge hotel.

I once saw the sun setting over the harbour. A haze shrouded the sun, but the scene was colourful in a delicate way, the harbour and houses being silhouetted against the restrained pastel tints of the sunset—the whole forming a picture at which a painter would have rejoiced. It was very quiet and peaceful, with little sound beyond the gentle fall of miniature waves. I walked to Dasher's Den, a rocky inlet near the foot of the cliffs to the south of the town. This is a place to avoid in heavy weather, as the sea then pours in with terrific force. Even on a calm evening it looks a sinister spot.

Portpatrick is only twenty-two miles away from the Mull of Galloway, but a leisurely day could be spent on the journey. This long narrow peninsula is known as the Rhinns of Galloway, and is honeycombed by a bewildering network of roads. It is a rich agricultural district of green fields, woods and prosperous farms famous for dairy herds. One's sense of direction plays strange tricks amongst the hills of the interior, and there are far too few signposts.

It is curiously exciting to drive down the narrow peninsula to the Mull. Much of the route lies on the east side of the Rhinns, along the shores of Luce Bay, but be sure to cut across to the western shores to visit Port Logan, famous for its fish-pond. A tidal pond full of tame cod-fish willing to eat out of your hand is a rare sight. But remember, the fish do not receive visitors on Tuesdays, Thursdays and Sundays.

Beyond Kirkmaiden and Broadwall the road rapidly deteriorates as it approaches the narrow isthmus between East and West Tarbet, which forms a natural gateway to the Mull of Galloway. I passed a delightful thatched and whitewashed cottage as spruce as a new pin. Even the rainwater tub was newly painted, and a friendly dog introduced me to the kindly old lady who lived at the cottage.

The Mull itself is a little more than a mile in length, and is approached by a road of singular vileness which twists like a snake near the edge of precipitous cliffs. Motorists are warned not to take their cars along this final stretch of road, but, as I had taken my car to Duncansby Head lighthouse at the extreme north-east of Scotland, I wanted to drive to the Mull of Galloway lighthouse, Scotland's south-western extremity. It would have been quicker to walk, and most people do. Nevertheless, I arrived after much low gear work and parked the car by the lighthouse. On clear days from the edge of the Mull there is a wonderful view, extending to Ireland, England, the Isle of Man, the Merrick and even Jura. I had a dizzy view of the cliffs and the sea over two hundred feet below, but the haze precluded further visibility. As a result I felt cut off from the world and gazed blankly at nothingness.

It was difficult to believe that this was as far south as the northern tip of Yorkshire. I set off for a walk along the edge of the cliffs, looking for a viewpoint which would show not only the lighthouse, but the bold outline of the Mull in addition. I found a good spot to the south-east of West Tarbet. It was a magnificent but frightening scene, and showed the exposed and remote situation of the lighthouse to great advantage. Yet there are far lonelier lighthouses on the Scottish seaboard, and it is often quite an adventure to reach some of them. The mighty cliffs extend several miles to the north-west of West Tarbet, and are a splendid sight.

It is well to allow plenty of time when visiting the Mull, and a good plan would be to take a picnic lunch, as the nearest hotel is at Drummore.

I bumped back to East Tarbet and passed Mull Farm near the Chapel of St. Medan, one of the oldest existing churches in Scotland. The recently excavated Candida Casa at Whithorn is, of course, a still older church.

After a late lunch at Drummore I went for a stroll around this tiny seaport. This is an odd part of Scotland, and would not seem out of place on

11

the north coast of Africa. It was just as hot, and I was continually reminded of a small Algerian seaport I once knew very well. Even the hotel was slightly bizarre, the interior decorations being quite distinctive. It is true that I missed the Arab children and the Algerian wine, and I certainly heard no French spoken; yet the impression persisted, and Luce Bay was quite as blue as the Mediterranean.

An absolutely straight and monotonous road leads from Sandhead to Glenluce, passing the Stranraer road near Dunragit. We digress to Castle Kennedy, approached by a by-road near the station. Extensive woods frame the shores of the White Loch, and you can look across the reed-fringed waters to the ivy-covered ruins of Castle Kennedy, resting in quiet dignity on a wooded peninsula. Away to the left the more modern Loch Inch Castle has all the appearance of some stately French château. The rough road leading round the White Loch to Castle Kennedy is a sheer delight, and an interesting extension encircles the Black Loch and rejoins the peninsula separating the two lochs at Loch Inch Castle. The carriage-drive rejoins the main road near Inch Church.

It is only thirty-five miles by sea from Stranraer to Larne, hence Stranraer is an important seaport, enjoying a sheltered situation at the head of Loch Ryan. The harbour station is at the end of a stone pier jutting about half a mile out to sea. The leisurely sweep of the harbour is not unattractive. Otherwise Stranraer has little of interest to the tourist apart from an old castle once used as a gaol. There is also an airport which attracts a good deal of traffic. In short, we are back in civilisation, and on the long coast road from Stranraer to the Firth of Clyde.

The road hugs the eastern shore of Loch Ryan to Cairn Ryan, beyond where the road climbs high above the water. There is often heavy traffic on this rather narrow, winding coastal road, so it is as well to stop in order to appreciate the view across to Milleur Point, the northernmost tip of the Rhinns of Galloway.

The road now turns inland and climbs steadily up the wooded slopes of Glen App, an attractive glen but one not seen to best advantage from the roadside. There are more satisfying views from the surrounding hills. On a clear, sunny evening you will not readily forget the scene from the descent

Dundrennan Abbey,
Kirkcudbrightshire

KIRKCUDBRIGHTSHIRE AND AYRSHIRE

Tam o' Shanter
Ayr

TURNBERRY AND AILSA CRAIG, AYRSHIRE

*Ailsa Craig
(1114 ft.)—f
the west, early
morning*

to Ballantrae, which reveals much of the coast to the north and the Stinchar Valley to the north-east. It is from here that you may obtain your first view of distant Ailsa Craig. There is something nebulous and unreal about this rocky islet, as though at any moment it might vanish like a puff of smoke. Yet it may well remain an almost constant companion during several days of travel, as it is visible from Arran, the Kintyre coast and much of the mainland. Its dominant shape draws ever nearer as we approach Girvan, and at times it seems to be so close that it is difficult to believe it is never nearer the coast than eight or nine miles.

Ballantrae, an unpretentious fishing village, is approached by a stone bridge across the mouth of the River Stinchar, and is overlooked by the ruins of Ardstinchar Castle. Beyond Ballantrae the road climbs steadily to the summit of Bennane Head, where you may enjoy wonderful views of the undulating Carrick coast to the north, golden sunsets seawards, and perhaps see Kintyre and Arran to the north-west, with our old friend Ailsa floating peacefully in the foreground. The popular coast road from Bennane Head to Lendalfoot, Kennedy's Pass and Girvan gives ever-changing pictures of rocky beaches, cliffs, distant hills, and, above all, the splendour of the sea. Kennedy's Pass is best seen on a breezy, sunny day at high water, when the waves are sending up clouds of spray as they break against the great rocks at the roadside.

Although this coast road is at no great height, it has been hewn between the rocks with dramatic effect. Here, you will find narrow coves bounded by a steeply shelving beach, guarded by great rocks. Sit here and watch the eager rush of the waves as they surge past, followed by attendant armies of spume; a myriad pinpoints of light flicker and scintillate as the sun shines serenely upon their troubled surface. But the outcome is always the same— a thunderous crash, clouds of stinging spray, and the sullen roar of hosts of pebbles in noisy protest. On such a day there is a magic about this place which will long linger in your memory.

You will like Girvan. It combines modern attractions with a fine harbour; it has a promenade where you can sit and look across the gateway to the Clyde; there are lovely sunsets, good hotels, many green open spaces along the front, a variety of shops and a cinema. But above all is an impression of freshness, as if the town had a scrub and polish at least twice a day; and there is always the distant fascination of Ailsa Craig. Some day you will be tempted to sail out to Ailsa and learn something of its mysteries.

It is a thrilling experience to approach Ailsa from the sea. Although only three quarters of a mile across, it is a fifth of a mile in height or, to be precise, 1114 feet, and once formed the core of a volcano. Precipitous cliffs rise from the sea to a height of 400 feet in places. From the top of the cliffs the gradient is steep to the summit of the isle, and the climb is laborious. Ailsa is the home of myriads of sea-fowl, still unused to the sound of ships' sirens. As we approached the island our siren hooted vigorously, and I was amazed to see an avalanche of sea-fowl fall from the cliffs and whirl into cloud-like formations. Tens of thousands of sea-gulls panicked at our approach, yet I was astonished to realise we were still some distance from the island.

It was evening and a heavy sea was running. The setting sun floodlit the island, and the great cliffs gleamed with a strange effulgence. It was a magnificent sight, and I have never seen Ailsa in such microscopic detail before or since. But the peculiar mystical quality of Ailsa is best seen very early in the morning when the top is scraping the clouds and wisps of mist trickle down the sides. Ailsa then seems shrouded with a ghostly halo, and seen against a silvery sky the effect is most eerie.

I remember Girvan harbour at high tide. The fishing-boats lay serene and content under the blazing sun, and scarcely a ripple disturbed the water. A group of art students were sketching the scene. A fisherman gazed thoughtfully across the harbour towards the slender spire of the church. Girvan was at peace, and I was very loth to disturb this tranquillity. I picked my way between the ropes and bollards, and crept silently northwards.

A golden sunset lay across Turnberry Bay, and I left the main road and walked down to the beach. The sea was in a quiet mood, and oily ripples reflected dazzling patches of light as they advanced leisurely towards me. A pall of dark clouds lay overhead, but gave way to golden clouds far out to sea. There was only the music of the water to break the silence, and I marvelled to find such solitude and splendour so near a busy main road.

It is twenty-two miles from Girvan to Ayr. Cars and coaches can make the journey quite comfortably in an hour, although you could spend a full day, and still not see all the attractions on this short route.

Turnberry lighthouse, near the scant ruins of Turnberry Castle, can be approached by a rough track skirting the famous golf-links. The lighthouse occupies a setting of great natural beauty at the top of a rocky windswept promontory looking across to Arran.

Another deviation should be made to the tiny fishing village of Maidens near the notorious Maiden Rocks which mount guard over Maidenhead Bay. A lengthy breakwater extends almost to the rocks, and you will pass many fishing nets hung out to dry.

Do not miss Culzean Castle. It is very gratifying to know that this wonderful estate is now the property of the National Trust. There are delightful walks through the wooded grounds as far as Maidenhead Bay, which has a quiet beach under the benign eye of Ailsa Craig. There is the Swan Pond where you will want to linger by cool, still waters. The castle is magnificent, and the landward side faces terraced gardens. The seaward side, built along a great cliff, is still more impressive. Built by Robert Adam in 1777, Culzean Castle features much of his finest work, including a superb oval stairway and a magnificent round drawing-room overlooking the Firth of Clyde. The best preserved Adam ceiling is in the Long Drawing Room, where you will also see an ornate French clock once belonging to the Empress Josephine. The armoury, library, and dining-room are also noteworthy. Two lower rooms are converted into restaurants. A suite at Culzean Castle is permanently reserved for the use of General Eisenhower.

The main road turns inland beyond Culzean, and continues to Maybole, but the coast road winds seawards again and emerges at a considerable height, giving distant views of the peaks of Arran. Near here you will meet with the Electric Brae, an odd roadside illusion giving the impression that you are ascending when descending and vice versa.

The railway is in the foreground and does much to detract from the view of Dunure Castle. This picturesque ruin can be approached by a narrow lane diverging from the main road. The road maintains a high level as far as the Heads of Ayr, where you can enjoy an extensive view of Ayr

15

Bay and Ayr. The way ahead is a fast main road, so look out for a branch road leading to Alloway.

A full afternoon could be spent at Alloway, where you will see the birthplace of Burns, a long, low, thatched cottage by the roadside, and the roofless shell of Alloway Kirk where Tam o' Shanter saw witches and warlocks. I enjoyed the scene best on a sunny afternoon when 'Alloway's auld haunted kirk' lay at peace. The sunlight through the trees cast shadows on the crumbling walls, and the tombstones stood drowsily in mute ranks.

The view from the parapet of the bridge across the Doon, looking up-stream towards the graceful sweep of the single arch of the Auld Brig o' Doon, is one of the fairest in Scotland. Walk to the high arch of the Auld Brig and admire the view back to the new bridge, dominated by the Burns Monument, a Grecian temple with nine columns. More Burns relics are housed in the Monument, where you can climb a circular staircase to the base of the temple, and thus obtain an unusual view of the Auld Brig in its wooded setting. Nor should you miss seeing the remarkable statues of Tam o' Shanter and Souter Johnnie.

Ayr is a large and prosperous town: very busy, very modern, yet con-taining much that is old. The quaint, thatched Tam o' Shanter Inn, the Wallace Tower and St. John's Tower (sometimes wrongly called Fort Castle) should be visited. Then it is worth walking across the New Bridge to see the Auld Brig which dates from the thirteenth century, and is now a footbridge. The Esplanade is a spacious road bordering extensive sands.

I cannot pretend to any great enthusiasm for the journey northwards, which, for the next few miles, is a peculiar combination of industrial Ayr-shire, modern holiday resorts and golf courses. Prestwick is famous not only for golf but for its airport. Connoisseurs of cafetaria will welcome the unusual Dutch House Restaurant near Monkton. Troon combines fine sands, more golf, good hotels and a busy harbour. The air is bracing and breezy. You can enjoy fine sunsets anywhere on the Clyde coast, and Troon is no ex-ception. At times the views across the water to Arran are very fine.

The broad sweep of the Irvine estuary is seen to advantage from the bridge at Irvine, and makes a rather impressive picture. Fast main roads bring us to Kilwinning and Stevenston. A by-pass from Stevenston avoids

...dens Pier,
...bour and rocks,
...shire

AYRSHIRE AND DUNBARTONSHIRE

...oudscape: Gare
...ch at Rhu,
...nbartonshire

*Loch Fyne from
Cairndow, look
S.W. (spring
morning)*

ARGYLL

*Cattle at Sadde
Kintyre*

Saltcoats and Ardrossan, but I like to make a point of visiting these places; after all, one should see all aspects of Scotland. Saltcoats is quite a popular watering place, and the busy docks at Ardrossan are full of interest. Many seaward views are obtained on the road northwards to West Kilbride, and for once the road has pride of place over the railway.

Largs is my favourite resort on the Ayrshire coast. I have mentioned my impression of Girvan having a scrub and polish twice daily. Largs gives a similar impression; it is an exceptionally clean and sparkling holiday resort, and owes much to its enviable situation opposite the island of Great Cumbrae, within sight of Bute and Arran. The town is sheltered beneath high hills.

Many steamer excursions are possible from Largs, and it is a port of call for various Clyde pleasure cruises. It is unquestionably a holiday resort, and several comfortable hotels cater for the needs of visitors. I think one may claim to see Highland sunsets from Largs, and as the sun sets over the distant mountains of Cowal we may experience our first real excitement on our long approach to the Western Highlands.

Whenever I am in Largs in fine weather I take the long winding climb towards Camphill Reservoir, and halt at a café which has a breathtaking view. A path leads from the café to a still higher viewpoint, and from here you have the world at your feet. The Firth of Clyde can be seen from Ailsa Craig to northern Cowal, and the islands of Arran, Bute and Cumbrae form a foreground to views of distant Kintyre. When there is a brilliant sunset this is a scene beyond description. It is not just the sheer magnificence of the view which attracts, but the evidence of life and activity in miniature. You can watch a toy train as it travels mile after mile along the coast. Cars appear no larger than pinheads, and steamers and other craft seem pathetically puny. Largs lies directly beneath, looking stately and regal with its tall spires, and the Clyde coast is a sheet of molten silver against the setting sun.

The Lowlands of Scotland are very fortunate in having roads following so much of the coastline. As we travel further into the Western Highlands we shall not find the coastline so easy of access.

If I had to choose the best stretch of Lowland coast road my choice would be the fourteen miles between Largs and Gourock. A fine, sparkling day is essential to enjoy the superb views across the narrowing Firth of Clyde—at times only two or three miles in width—and the magnificent mountain scenery of Arran and Cowal is in sharp contrast to the gentle Renfrew hills. If the day should be breezy with brilliant clouds the scene is even more colourful. I have seen this stretch of the Clyde many times. During the war I spent hours at a time surveying the scene from the high vantage point of a battleship look-out post. On one such occasion, when sailing for West Africa, I had an almost aerial view as we sailed down the Firth of Clyde. It was a day of sheer perfection, and my feelings on leaving such a scene for a very bleak future can well be imagined. It was an exhilarating experience to return to these beloved landmarks after the shadow of war had lifted.

The coast road becomes even more agreeable as we approach Inverkip and the Cloch lighthouse. The road itself is wide and has a first-class surface, and one drives 'on velvet', with the many trees supplying just the right touch of foreground.

On a clear day at the Cloch lighthouse the houses of Dunoon, though two miles distant, seem little more than a stone's throw away. If the Clyde were bridged, Dunoon could be reached in a few minutes; as it is, the road journey by car from Cloch to Dunoon is not far short of one hundred miles.

There are good views of the Holy Loch, Loch Long and the Rosneath peninsula as we continue to Gourock, a popular resort directly opposite Kilcreggan. But once Gourock is behind, the next few miles will show a very different aspect of Scotland as we drive through the great shipbuilding centres of Greenock and Port Glasgow. I think it is a great mistake for the tourist to avoid entirely the grimmer and sterner aspects of the Scottish scene. It is true that there are large areas in mid-Scotland which are dull and drab, but somehow this does not seem to apply to Greenock. There is always a note of adventure about places where ships are born, and dock-yards have an interest not readily appreciated.

CHAPTER THREE

GREENOCK TO DUNOON

GREENOCK, birthplace of James Watt and Captain Kidd, teems with life and activity. Its busy shipyards and engineering works occupy much of the Clyde coastline and merge into Port Glasgow, formerly Glasgow's harbour before the Clyde was made suitable for major shipping. You will get a much better view of this intriguing district if you climb high into the hills to the south. You can then see this busy industrial area spread out like a carpet beneath your feet, and bounded by the amazingly indented Clyde coast. It is a wonderful view, including Dunoon, Holy Loch, Loch Long, Gare Loch and the Clyde estuary towards the Rock of Dumbarton.

You can cross the Clyde at Erskine Ferry, which avoids the necessity of a long detour towards Glasgow. At this point the Clyde is barely a quarter of a mile across, and forms a natural division between Highlands and Lowlands. Scotland is divided into separate scenic compartments: the Clyde and the Firth of Forth guard the Southern Lowlands, and the Caledonian Canal separates the North-western from the Central Highlands. The Western Highlands continue southwards from Oban to Kintyre, and are neatly separated from the Lowlands by the Firth of Clyde. The main compartments have many lesser compartments all neatly sealed away from each other, such as the Kingdom of Fife and the Rhinns of Galloway.

Once you have crossed the Erskine Ferry and turned westwards you have entered the attractive land of mountains and lochs, seen with increasing interest on our long journey up the Clyde coast.

It would be a pity, however, to omit Glasgow from our itinerary, and thus miss Britain's second largest city and Scotland's most populous town and largest seaport. It would be invidious to compare Glasgow with Edinburgh. The two places are totally different in character, and you must not expect to find a tourists' Mecca in Glasgow. The romance, the beauty and the historical glamour of Edinburgh have but little equivalent in Glasgow, essentially a great industrial city with emphasis on shipbuilding and vast chemical, engineering and iron works. It is very much the big city, teeming with life and activity, so modern in fact that there is not much of the past left to see. It is true that we should visit Provand's Lordship, built in 1471, and furnished in early eighteenth-century style; and the magnificent thirteenth-century cathedral, the only undamaged Gothic church in the Lowlands; but for the rest we must look to more recent achievements.

To my mind the finest view in Glasgow is the celebrated scene 'doon the watter' from the King George V Bridge overlooking the Broomielaw. The history of the Clyde and its steamers makes one of the greatest industrial romances of all time.

If time permits you really ought to visit the sumptuous City Chambers, the fascinating Art Gallery and Museum, the dignified and imposing University and the Hunterian Museum and Library. To do even this much you will need to stay in Glasgow a while, but it is a friendly city where you will be made very welcome.

St. Mungo is the patron saint of Glasgow, and you will find some of his miracles featured in the city arms. He was a contemporary of St. Columba who visited him from distant Iona. Nothing is left of his chapel, or at least no remains have been found, but the traditional grave of the saint can be seen in the cathedral crypt.

If you want a glimpse of the shipbuilding areas your westbound route may be along busy Argyle Street and Dumbarton Road, but the preferable route from the traffic viewpoint is by way of Western Road. Both routes converge at Old Kilpatrick near the north side of the Erskine Ferry, where we can continue to Dumbarton. Both Old Kilpatrick and Dumbarton claim to be the birthplace of St. Patrick (373-463), but Dumbarton with its great rock—the Dun Breton or 'Hill of the Britons'—hoary with antiquity, would seem the more probable place.

Dumbarton is a crowded industrial town with shipbuilding yards. The chief interest is the castle built on a great isolated mass of rock, so conspicuous from Langbank on the opposite shore of the Clyde.

The main road avoids the castle, which must be approached by rather grimy streets leading towards the Clyde. An extensive clearing is reached in the vicinity of the huge basaltic rock. There are seats on the green, and pleasant views across the estuary. The ascent to the top of the rock involves a climb of about 240 feet but the view is well worth the trouble.

Another interesting scene is from the bridge across the Leven estuary at Dumbarton; the rock is seen from the rear, and its twin humps appear strangely incongruous where one would expect to find the low-lying banks of a river estuary.

The Clyde is nearly four miles wide at Helensburgh, directly opposite Greenock. Helensburgh has a fine esplanade, and is a busy and popular resort within easy reach of Loch Lomond.

The coast road follows the eastern shore of the Gare Loch to Rhu, Shandon and Garelochhead. The many views across to the Rosneath peninsula are hampered at times by an extraordinary miscellany of unwanted shipping, giving the Gare Loch the appearance of a parking ground for careworn vessels. Garelochhead is, as the name implies, situated at the head of the loch, and its setting is undeniably attractive, the approach to it being heralded by a row of venerable trees by the lochside.

There is a long climb from Garelochhead over to Whistlefield, and it is worth stopping near the top to look back at the extensive view of the Gare Loch and the distant Clyde. Due to the untidy clutter of shipping, the view is more interesting than picturesque. The entire length of the Rosneath peninsula can be seen. Loch Goil and Loch Long are prominent to the west, and the entrance to Loch Goil is almost directly beneath, where it joins Loch Long. But the view I like best is from a hill-top near the roadside just before the descent to Loch Long. The upper reaches of this long, narrow loch are seen extending towards Arrochar, with richly wooded slopes on one side and Argyll's Bowling Green on the other. This is a mountain park forming part of the Argyll National Forest Park. Henceforth we shall see many lochs, and this first impressive view, covering much of Loch Long, is characteristic. This little hill is between the road and the loch, and it is only a short stroll to the top. I feel that if you have come thus far, you will not rest until you have explored the scenic paradise to which this is but the gateway.

The road to Arrochar is pleasant for the passenger, but a bit tiresome for the driver. It is a narrow, winding main road, well-wooded and picturesque as it keeps close to the edge of the loch; but it is no road for day dreaming.

Arrochar, situated at the head of Loch Long and within a mile and a half of Loch Lomond, must be unrivalled as a centre for gatherings of the tourist clans. The Arrochar hills, particularly the Cobbler and Narnain, attract climbers; cyclists, hikers and coaches arrive in their myriads; steamers disgorge a further flood of trippers, and even the railway delivers its quota. I have often wondered how Arrochar absorbs this vast itinerant population without bursting. The three main hotels must have an unending struggle to cope with the crowd. I have never known Arrochar quiet even during off-season periods; no doubt there are times, perhaps in mid-winter, when the place has time to take a deep breath and try to recapture some semblance of its pristine peace.

Although this is a book on the western seaboard, I do not intend that we should march along the beach from the Mull of Galloway to Cape Wrath. Therefore I make no apology for a digression to Loch Lomond, which, at Tarbet, is less than one and a half miles from the sea. If you are staying at Arrochar, an excellent circular trip is to go to Tarbet and take the road south to Luss and Ross Park, and then cut across to Helensburgh, returning via Gare Loch and Loch Long.

A main road closely hugs the shores of the entire west bank of Loch Lomond from Balloch to Ardlui, and we join it at Tarbet. This is probably the most popular tourist route in the whole of Scotland, but unfortunately the road was never built to sustain such traffic. The surface is good, but the road is narrow and very winding; you are sure to meet long processions of cars, and if you do experience a sudden lull, prepare for a heavy lorry at the next corner. Unless you can arise at the crack of dawn, eternal vigilance is the price of using this busy road. Given fine weather the scenery is magnificent, and your passengers can have unending enjoyment as the twenty-five mile lochside journey is consistently picturesque. If I had to select some favourite halting place on this scenic journey, I should choose the model village of Luss, and walk down the village street to the pier. The cottages are neat and trim, and each has its little flower garden; in some cases the walls are flower festooned; elsewhere the road is bordered with well-kept low hedges, with cottages and gardens on either side. The view from the pier is of great beauty. The northern aspect is guarded by Ben Lomond, and the many islands of the loch can be seen to the east and the south. The scene is enriched by woods which are as yet unspoiled. You are sure to see a cluster of boats drawn up on the shore; sometimes the waters of the loch are sparkling and rippling; at other times I have seen great waves which would not have disgraced the sea; but the surface is often as still as glass until disturbed by some passing swan; on the cool breeze of evening you may sometimes smell wood smoke.

If you wish to get away from crowds of visitors, and are prepared to travel a considerable distance, there is a quiet by-road along the east bank of the loch as far as the hotel at Rowardennan. This road can be reached by driving to Balloch, Drymen and Balmaha, where you will find a pier, a café, and a charming view across to the island of Inchcailloch. The road passes through exquisite scenery between Balmaha and Rowardennan, and extensive views of the loch can be enjoyed at leisure.

The motoring road ends at Rowardennan, and cars must return all the way to Drymen, but a rough track extends to Rowardennan and Ptarmigan Lodges. The former is now a Youth Hostel, and enjoys one of the finest situations in the Highlands. I walked there one sunny morning before breakfast, and was quite enchanted with the place. Although it was so early there were several children playing about on the velvet lawn by the lochside, climbers were getting ready with great cheerfulness for a day on Ben Lomond, and one stalwart was busy cleaning an immense pile of boots. The outlook across the water to the wooded heights of Glen Douglas, seen in the freshness of morning, the beauty of the loch itself placidly washing against the gentle shores, the sense of remoteness from the busy road on the opposite side of the loch, all these built up a picture which bordered on the sublime.

Rowardennan is the best starting point for the ascent of Ben Lomond, a climb well worth the effort for the sake of the immense panorama from the top.

The only other road touching the east bank of Loch Lomond approaches from the Trossachs and descends to the water level at Inversnaid, where you will find falls, a comfortable hotel and some delightful local walks, perhaps the best being the lochside walk to the north leading to Rob Roy's Cave.

Loch Lomond is twenty miles in length as the crow flies, but the winding road from Balloch to Ardlui covers fully twenty-five miles. The steamers cover about twenty-four miles, allowing for calls at the various piers. Excluding Ireland, Loch Lomond is Britain's largest freshwater loch, and, although only 23 feet above sea level, attains a depth of 623 feet. The sea at Arrochar, little more than a mile distant from Tarbert, is not nearly so deep; in fact the upper reaches of Loch Long are less than a third as deep. Bearing in mind Loch Lomond's reputation for sudden squalls and choppy surface, the safest and easiest way to explore its waters is by steamer. There are services along the full length of the loch from Balloch to Ardlui, calling at Balmaha, Luss, Rowardennan and Tarbet.

But our course lies to the west, and the Inveraray road is followed as far as Rest and Be Thankful. There has been much road reconstruction in this part of the world, and the road from Arrochar to Inveraray, Dalmally and Oban is now one of the best in Scotland. The road winds round the head of Loch Long as far as Glencroe, a wild and savage glen dominated by the steep slopes of The Cobbler, The Brack, Ben Ime and Ben Donich. The main road used to follow a steep and winding course with a mildly exciting bend near the top of Rest and Be Thankful; now a completely new road has been built and the ascent is very gradual but much less interesting.

The old road remains for the walker, and to remind us of pre-war days when cars used to reach the summit of Rest and Be Thankful with boiling engines, and both driver and car rested and were thankful. The new hill is little more than a gentle stroll, although a long one. But the view from the top down wild Glencroe is still nearly the same magnificent prospect, and the scar of the new road has been made as inconspicuous as possible. This view is at its best on a day of crystal clarity, when every detail of the mountains is sharply defined, and The Cobbler broods in rocky content.

Nearing the foot of Glen Kinglass we enter Cowal, and leave the fast main road which sweeps round Loch Fyne to Inveraray. Most of the roads in Cowal are singularly free of traffic, and it is generally possible to tour the entire district in peace and comfort. The approach to Cowal is quite impressive. Immediately after leaving the busy main road in Glen Kinglass we descend into a wooded ravine spanned by a tall and solid stone bridge. The descent is made by characteristic hairpin bends, which give fair warning that we are now in a district of rather tricky, if picturesque, roads. There is a good view of Loch Fyne, 'The Bright Water', winding its serpentine way towards the mountains around Glen Fyne. Loch Fyne, about fifty miles in length, must be one of the longest sea lochs in Scotland. A quiet coast road leads from St. Catherine's to Strachur. It seems strange to be at the seaside so far inland. The road keeps close to the shore, giving fine views across the loch to Inveraray, some two miles distant by sea.

I once drove southwards to Loch Eck on a very peaceful evening. Great clouds drifted across the mountains cradling the serene waters of the loch, and a golden sunset was making a desperate effort to break through the swirling mist. The scene was so lovely that I left the car and strolled along the shore of this solitary loch. The water was calm and untroubled, and the ripples reflected the golden light from the sunset. I looked across to Glen Bernice as the sun broke through for a brief instant, only to withdraw behind another swirling cloud and suffuse the scene with a strange ethereal light.

It was dusk as I rounded the Holy Loch and came to Kirn and Dunoon. If you have driven to Dunoon you will arrive with a sense of achievement; the hundred-mile journey from the Cloch lighthouse to Dunoon is not accomplished without effort. It is a queer feeling to have travelled so far and done no more than circumvent a two-mile sea crossing, but the hundred-mile detour will still be worth while, even when the proposed car ferries have made it unnecessary. It is a journey full of interest, and it will introduce you to some of the loveliest touring country in the Highlands.

CHAPTER FOUR

COWAL, BUTE AND ARRAN

Few writers have much to say about Cowal, although it is an excellent miniature of almost all types of Scottish scenery. It is a land of sea lochs whose remote reaches penetrate far inland and seek shelter beneath the rugged slopes of lofty mountains. There are bewildering changes of scene within short distances. Cowal is a hilly district, and therein lies the secret of its charm. Most surprising of all is the feeling of solitude geographically so near to Glasgow. There are parts of Cowal where you do really feel that you have escaped from the crowds and turmoil of the great world so near; you can find complete solitude, and bask in a peaceful, restful atmosphere away from all worry and care. Such places can be found within a very short distance of Dunoon.

Do not take Dunoon for granted because of its easy access by sea. With the exception of Oban and possibly Fort William, I know of no other popular Scottish holiday resort within such easy reach of sea and moorland, mountain and glen. It is also an admirable centre for short cruises to such places as Arran, Kintyre, Inveraray, the Kyles of Bute, the Ayr and Renfrew coast, and even Glasgow.

If you are favoured with a fine sunny evening, make the short drive from Holy Loch to Toward Point and Loch Striven, in the hope of a colourful sunset at the end of your journey. The Holy Loch is a peaceful and restful sight when white yachts are at anchor. There is a fine promenade from Sandbank to Hunter's Quay and Kirn, places which are practically northern extensions of Dunoon. You will see familiar scenes from a new viewpoint, including Kilcreggan on the Rosneath peninsula, Gourock and the friendly Cloch lighthouse. It is difficult to realise that Dunoon is not an island.

There is not much left of the thirteenth century Dunoon Castle, but the views of the Clyde estuary make the short walk worth while. The esplanade leads southwards, passing many hotels and houses with colourful gardens, and reaches Innellan and Toward Point. This is the southernmost tip of eastern Cowal, guarded by a lighthouse and a small breakwater, giving a widespread view of the blue expanse of the Clyde and the houses of Wemyss Bay and Skelmorlie as they catch the light of the evening sun.

The coast road now runs westwards to within two miles of Rothesay on the Isle of Bute. One must admit that the Scottish mainland makes many gallant attempts to reach the western islands, and Cowal completely surrounds the northern half of Bute.

After turning inland for three or four miles, we rejoin the sea on the shores of Loch Striven at a little place called Gortanansaig, directly opposite the Kyles of Bute. If you have a car you will be tempted to come here night after night and halt by this seaweed-strewn shore to watch the sunsets, and listen to the gentle lapping of the waves. A passing flock of sheep may complete a picture of rare charm.

A narrow road continues northwards alongside the shore for several miles, but just fails to connect with the main Sandbank-Glendaruel highway. As a result, motorists must retrace their route all the way to Dunoon; but the journey is equally attractive in either direction.

Our next excursion is on a much grander scale, and covers some of the loneliest and loveliest districts in Cowal. Just north of the Holy Loch the only road westwards deviates from the main road to the north, and winds through an attractive valley to Clachaig. Progress is slow, as the road follows a tortuous course among the foothills separating Glen Lean from the head of Loch Striven. On the descent to Lochhead, the narrow winding road enters some very lovely country around the head of the loch. A steep climb beyond Craigendaive leads to a lofty viewpoint where you can see Loch Striven stretching towards Inverchaolain and Gortanansaig. The wooded slopes of the east bank of the loch are quite precipitous. It is amazing to find such solitude within easy reach of busy Dunoon. The road to Glen Lean looks very forlorn threading its way up fern-clad foothills.

As we approach Glendaruel, new attractions unfold in every direction. The sparkling blue waters of Loch Ridden will tempt you southwards to Colintraive, approached by a narrow lane giving delightful views of the Kyles of Bute.

Colintraive is a sheltered resort with a restful, sleepy atmosphere where time seems meaningless. Except for a brief interval when a visiting steamer called at the pier with its cargo of passengers there was little activity. Now that even this practice has ceased, the only excitement is the car ferry across to Rudhabodach in Bute. But this was not always so. The Kyles attain their narrowest span at Colintraive, hence this was the point where cattle were forded across to Bute when returning from the Argyllshire markets, thus giving rise to the name 'Caol an t'anaimh' or 'The Straits of the Swimming'.

In order to reach Glendaruel you will have to return to the main road and continue westwards. The road descends to where the River Ruel meanders placidly between lush green banks, where contented sheep will scarcely look up from their grazing as you pass by. This is a good spot for a picnic, but you may prefer the cosy hotel nestling at the foot of Glendaruel.

Although Cowal receives scant mention in Scottish books, the motoring press is apt to call attention to a mountain road which climbs from Ballochandrain near Kilmodan in Glendaruel, and in less than two miles ascends from sea level to a height of 1042 feet, before descending to Otter Ferry on Loch Fyne side. This hill merits respect for its length, its zigzag bends and its one-in-four gradient. On one visit to Cowal I drove up here. My only anxiety during the long ascent was due to a high grass-covered ridge in the centre of the narrow road, and this polished the undercarriage of the car as clean as a new pin. But I could never be quite sure the ridge would be content with mere polishing, and a concealed boulder or two would have made short work of my tour.

Despite a slight haze on the top I could see the delicate tracery of the Argyll mountains far beyond the outline of Loch Fyne. There was no sound beyond the gentle soughing of the wind and the occasional bleat of a sheep. The glorious moorland air, laden with the scent of the heather, and the tang of the distant sea, had a truly exhilarating quality.

I cautiously descended to Otter Ferry, scraping over the tufts and bumping into the pot-holes of this adventurous road. Otter Ferry must be one of the loneliest places in Cowal. Every prospect is perfect, and one can stand on the lonely quay as I did, and hear nothing beyond the quiet lapping of the waters of Loch Fyne. I looked across an expanse of incredibly blue water towards the gentle hills of south Knapdale. The Lochgilphead road was two miles distant on the opposite shore, but nearly sixty miles distant by road. This will give some idea of the length of this great sea-loch, but even at Otter Ferry I was many miles from where it meets the sea.

My route now lay northwards along one of the most fascinating roads in Cowal. It is an adventurous road, and continues for mile after mile alongside the extreme edge of Loch Fyne, and steering a car requires some care. The charm and brilliance of the route are best appreciated on a clear, sunny day when billowing picture-clouds sail across the sky. This was another grass-grown road, and but for the evidence of my maps I should have wondered if the road would terminate in a footpath—a distressing feature of many remote lochside roads in the Western Highlands. I came at length to Castle Lachlan, seat of the old Loch Fyne family of Maclachlan. The road made a short detour inland up Strathlachlan, but later rejoined the coast at Newton Bay.

If you like adventurous roads and magnificent scenery there is nothing insuperable about this route, and you can return from Strachur to Dunoon by Loch Eck and Whistlefield. But if you have time, follow the narrow, steep hill-road climbing past Whistlefield Hotel and over the hills to Ardentinny. Stop at the top to see the views of Loch Eck to the north and Glen Finart to the south-east. Extensive afforestation has added warmth to the scene, and the trees do not detract from the view. The road descends very steeply between high fern-clad banks, and you can see Loch Long in the distance.

Ardentinny is a small and unspoiled resort with charming views of Loch Long and the Rosneath peninsula. There are attractive walks in the neighbourhood, perhaps the best being to Lochgoilhead. You can sit on the pebbly beach at Ardentinny and look across to Coulport, two miles distant, by sea and seventy miles away by road. Motorists accustomed to touring in England will have many surprises in store when they calculate road distances in the Western Highlands. Such immense detours should be welcomed on a touring holiday, as they involve travel through delightful scenery which might otherwise be missed. You are not encouraged to hurry in Cowal.

The road to Dunoon encircles Strone Point, another well-known Clyde viewpoint. From here you will see the great sweep of Loch Long to the north, Holy Loch and Kirn to the west and much of the Renfrew coast to the south. But the best view is looking eastwards towards the sparkling white houses of Kilcreggan, the more distant houses of Gourock and the immense Clyde estuary sweeping towards Dumbarton and beyond.

Cowal has still further attractions to offer, and a leisurely day can be spent driving to Glendaruel and along the narrow lane beside the west bank of Loch Ridden as far as Ormidale Lodge, where the road ends. From this point a path leads southwards to Glen Caladh Castle and Tighnabruaich alongside the Kyles of Bute, a walk of rare beauty. But you will have to return the same way to Glendaruel for the next stage of our journey.

Our route now lies northwards up the fertile valley of the Ruel, which gradually narrows to form a typical, richly-wooded Scottish glen. The road climbs steadily, and the woods give way to moorland. Halt near the top and look back to one of the finest views in Cowal. For once there is no glimpse of sea or loch. The narrow white ribbon of road, with its grass ridge in the middle, can be seen for miles as it follows a winding course through the wide sweep of the hills.

When visibility is good the view northwards from the long descent to Loch Fyne is even more extensive, and includes the long range of hills between Loch Fyne and Loch Awe and the mountains of Jura beyond the hills of Knapdale to the south-west.

We can continue to Newton, Strachur and St. Catherine's to reach one of the few remaining Cowal roads which we still have to visit. The road climbs steeply from Loch Fyne side to Hell's Glen, and there is a bird's-eye view of Inveraray from the top. This is a lonely and rather bleak spot. The scenery improves as the glen becomes more wooded, and at the road junction at Monevechadan the River Goil is reached, and lends added interest to a scene of rugged, mountain grandeur. Lochgoilhead occupies a dreamlike situation, cradled at the head of the loch beneath towering mountains.

I remember standing on the pier, absorbing the dreamy, sleepy, timeless quality of the scene. A trim yacht lay neatly berthed at the quayside. Cloud shadows drifted across the slopes of Ben Donich, and the breeze ruffled the surface of the loch into a myriad wrinkles. The hotel, the church and a row of houses lay sparkling white in the sunlight. A little girl was paddling somewhat diffidently on the pebbly beach. The drowsy peacefulness of the scene remains in my memory to this day.

Return to Monevechadan and follow the Glencroe road through wild and impressive mountain scenery until quite suddenly you look down on Rest and Be Thankful, and see the familiar view of Glencroe and The Cobbler. This surprise view completes our tour of Cowal by car, but we must return to Dunoon to sample some of the more attractive sea-trips.

Although I prefer to wander along a coastline rather than watch it drift past from a ship, I derive much pleasure from cruising as a supplementary mode of travel. In this way one can see long stretches of lonely coast not accessible from the land by any road or track. The cruise round the Kyles of Bute will restfully show us much that we have previously seen by difficult land routes. Call at Tighnabruaich, a quiet resort on the western side of the Kyles of Bute, and walk to Kames, Millhouse and Ascog, where you can look across Loch Fyne to Tarbert in Kintyre. A still more pleasant walk is from Auchenlochan to Tighnabruaich and along the shore to Port Driseach, where you can follow a most delightful footpath alongside the Kyles towards Glen Caladh Castle and Loch Ridden. If you have time it would be possible to continue to Ormidale and Glendaruel.

Rothesay is the main port of call on Bute, an island fifteen miles in length and three miles in breadth. Here you will find cinemas, concert parties, dance halls and, inevitably, large crowds of holiday makers. The town is well placed at the head of Rothesay Bay, and the promenade extends east to Craigmore and west to Ardbeg and Port Bannatyne, giving good views of the Clyde and Loch Striven.

I have very pleasant recollections of a recent visit to Bute. As I sailed down the Firth of Clyde on a sparkling summer morning, Dunoon looked especially inviting. The long promenade with its colourful houses, the distant cloud-capped Cowal hills, the blue waters of the Clyde ruffled by a strong breeze and the swoop of seagulls, all these made a picture I was sorry to leave. Rothesay Bay was not lacking in attraction either, and we arrived at the pier in time to allow a walk to Port Bannatyne and back before lunch.

Few promenade walks can be so attractive as this, and the stroll round Ardbeg Point gave splendid views of Loch Striven.

My plan was to travel as far south as possible by bus, and then walk to Glencallum Bay. I had time to visit Rothesay Castle, hidden away in the old part of the town. This is a very ancient castle going back to the eleventh century, and is said to have been founded by Magnus Barefoot. The castle was destroyed with customary thoroughness in the seventeenth century, but there is still enough left to merit a visit.

The Kilchattan bus was no luxury coach, and there was no dallying by the wayside. Bus drivers are often singularly hard-hearted about my frequent desire to stop for half an hour to take photographs or visit some local beauty spot, and I usually try to bow to the inevitable and resign myself to seeing lovely views flash by while bumping along to some journey's end.

Kilchattan has a pier, and it is only a short trip by steamer to Millport on Great Cumbrae.

The recently opened car-ferry from Colintraive to Rudhabodach now makes Bute much more accessible to the motorist, and there is much worth seeing. The magnificent mansion of Mountstuart, seat of the Marquis of Bute, can sometimes be visited by permit. The crumbling ruins of St. Blane's Chapel, near the southern tip of the island, invite exploration. The remains of the nave and chancel of this ancient chapel are still to be seen and are probably eleventh century, being founded upon the site of a still older chapel dating back to St. Blane in the sixth century.

The extreme south of Bute is full of interest, and there are magnificent views of the Isle of Arran, barely six miles distant. The only road to the south-west of the island beyond Kingarth is hilly and adventurous, but even this ends at Garrochy, and you must walk the half mile to Garroch Head. North of Kingarth, Bute is encircled by roads which give many views of sea and coast, but there is still no road round the extreme north of the island.

Although the highest hill on Bute is only 911 feet, you can still see

Plate 14. Early morning on Loch Lomond near Rowardennan

mountain panoramas. There are many places where the sea is invisible, but the scene is dominated by the peaks of Arran, and we have the odd effect of one island forming part of the scenery of another. Bute is also quite capable of borrowing scenery from Cowal in places where the narrow Kyles cannot be seen, with the result that it appears a much larger island than it actually is.

Loch Fad is the most interesting and largest of several inland lochs, and its northern reaches extend almost to Rothesay. Ettrick Bay, on the west of Bute, attracts many visitors from Rothesay, and despite the crowds you will not readily forget a sunset over Arran seen from this sandy bay. The southernmost tip of Cowal, Ardlamont Point, is almost directly opposite. It is an attractive drive to Port Bannatyne, round Kames Bay passing Kames Castle, and alongside the Kyles of Bute to the new car-ferry across to Colintraive. Another grand route is from Ettrick Bay to Kilmichael opposite Kames, and it is a pity that this road does not continue right round northern Bute.

The island of Arran is very different in character to Bute. Although further south, it is much more mountainous, and Goat Fell is only one of many fine peaks. There are many difficult rock climbs, but it is an easy walk to the summit of Goat Fell. The best approach to Arran is from Ardrossan, but other popular though longer approaches are from Dunoon, Gourock and Rothesay. Cars may be ferried across from Ardrossan.

The contrast between the Highland scenery of Arran and the typical Lowland country around Ardrossan is amazing. When you land at Brodick you step into a new world, and were it not for the distant views of the mainland it would be hard to believe that Arran, whose magnificent scenery and mountains attract many visitors, occupies such an easily accessible situation in the Firth of Clyde.

On a recent visit to Arran I had the good fortune to see the hills in fine weather. Visibility was excellent. I had booked a passage on a coach tour of the northern half of the island, and was more or less resigned to the fact that many beautiful scenes would escape my camera. The entire route gave

Plate 15. Firth of Lorne: sunset from Connel, Argyll

magnificent views of glen and mountain, sea and village. The wooded policies of Brodick Castle, the cottages at Corrie and the impressive view of Glen Sannox made me long for the opportunity to stop and see them at leisure.

We drove up North Glen Sannox and descended to Glen Chalmadale. The coach stopped at a café, giving me the chance to walk to Loch Ranza and see the castle, and it was worth missing a meal to walk in such delightful surroundings. The village, loch and castle of Loch Ranza are picturesque even by Arran standards. On one side the hills sweep down to the row of houses on the waterfront. The tall, square shape of the fourteenth century Loch Ranza Castle dominates a promontory projecting from the pebbly beach. It was low water, several boats lay high and dry on the foreshore, and the Kintyre coast could be seen some five miles to the west. I had just time to walk round the castle before a plaintive hooting from the bus told me that the driver had been counting his passengers and had found one missing. Beyond Loch Ranza the coast road kept very close to the shore, giving colourful views of the Kintyre coast from Skipness to Saddell.

We returned to Brodick over the 'String' Pass. The view from the top looking down Glen Shurig to Brodick Bay was so outstanding that I managed to persuade the driver to stop the coach while I took a hurried photograph. We returned to Brodick after a most agreeable tour of nearly forty miles. Another circular tour of similar length takes in the southern half of the island, visiting Lamlash, Kildonan Castle and Blackwater, again returning by way of the 'String' Pass. Another road crosses the island from Sliddery to Lamlash via Glen Scorrodale. The remainder of the island can best be seen by the climber and walker, although many wonderful distant views can be enjoyed from the sea and the adjacent mainland. In particular, the majestic view of Holy Isle, towering above Lamlash Bay, is impressive from every direction.

If you want a Highland holiday in the Firth of Clyde, go to Arran. It is a little world in itself, and its accessibility does not make it any less enjoyable.

CHAPTER FIVE

DUNOON TO KINTYRE, KNAPDALE AND OBAN

IT is interesting to note how the mainland of Scotland reaches out to the islands. Most of the Inner Hebrides are visible from the extremity of some mainland promontory, and even the Outer Hebrides can be seen at times.

The peninsula of Kintyre, beginning at Tarbert, is separated from Knapdale by an isthmus barely a mile wide, and extends southwards, keeping to the west of Cowal, Bute and the whole of Arran. The Mull of Kintyre, only thirteen miles from the coast of Ireland, reaches nearly as far south as Girvan on the Ayrshire coast. The Highland character persists to the last, but you will find it very hard to believe that Kintyre is on the mainland, so strong is the impression that you are on an island—much more so than when touring Bute or even Arran.

Our first objective is Ardrishaig, about twenty miles west of Dunoon, although roughly sixty-seven miles by road. The northbound route from Dunoon brings us to Strachur, St. Catherine's and Glen Kinglass, where we join the Inveraray road and continue towards the head of Loch Fyne. It is sixty miles from Strachur to Tarbert, and the entire route is by Loch Fyne side, most of the distance embracing its western shores. The head of Loch Fyne is so far inland that it seems incongruous to observe seaweed in the heart of Argyll, and to realise that we are still on Scotland's western seaboard.

The moment you cross the River Fyne, by the massive stone bridge, you are en route for Dunderave Castle, Neil Munro's 'Doom Castle'. Actually it is more of a tall tower than a stately stronghold, and rises abruptly from velvety lawns surrounded by trees which effectively hide it from the road. The castle dates from the sixteenth century and was restored in 1912. A quaint inscription over a doorway reads:

'I Man, Behald the end, Be not Vyser nor the Biestes. I hoip in God.'

There is a particularly fine view of Inveraray Castle from the ornate bridge across the Aray. The castle is square in shape with a round turreted tower at each corner and a massive tower in the centre. It is open to the public, and is situated in rich park-like grounds with some of the finest trees in Scotland nearby. One silver fir is 168 feet high, while a Scots pine is 128 feet.

Inveraray is guarded by richly-wooded hills, the most conspicuous being Duniquoich, surmounted by a tower, forming an admirable viewpoint. I have visited Inveraray many times, and have always come under its strange spell. Here you will find a pier, a tall church, an Iona Cross, whitewashed houses and other buildings, two or three hotels and a curious triple archway over the road, giving to the town a rather foreign appearance. But Inveraray has a peculiar brooding atmosphere as if it were living in days gone by—and undoubtedly it has a past. James of the Glen was tried here for the Appin murder. Dr Johnson and Boswell stayed at the Argyll Arms Hotel facing the quay, subsequently dining with the Duke and Duchess of Argyll at the Castle. The late Neil Munro was a native of the town, and if you would know more about this district the many books he wrote will take you into a dim and distant age as troubled as it was fascinating.

The long drive beside Loch Fyne to Lochgilphead and Ardrishaig gives many glimpses across to Cowal, which awaken memories of our recent visit.

Although the Crinan Canal passes close to the quiet little town of Lochgilphead, it does not join the sea until reaching Ardrishaig, considerably further down the lochside. The reason for this is fairly obvious when you look across the rather dreary expanse of mud and pebbles exposed at low water in the upper reaches of Loch Gilp. We shall see more of the little-used Crinan Canal on our return northwards from Kintyre.

The road to Tarbert hugs the shore and, due to a comparatively straight coastline, runs directly southwards. But Loch Fyne is still with us, and begins to narrow as we approach Tarbert.

First impressions of Tarbert are of an untidy cluster of houses and a tangle of small fishing boats in a harbour overlooked by the ruins of an ancient castle, once occupied by Bruce.

It is only a mile from East Loch Tarbert to West Loch Tarbert, hence

*...aks of Arran
...m above
...enreasdell,
...ntyre*

ARRAN AND OBAN

*...an from Pulpit
...—stormy
...set*

Loch Awe from Port Sonachan

ARGYLL

Inveraray on June morning, Loch Fyne

Kintyre is very nearly an island. In 1093 Magnus Barefoot decided that Kintyre *should* be an island. He had been ceded the Western Isles and thought he would like to add Kintyre to his collection. Consequently he had himself drawn in his galley across the narrow isthmus and thus having 'sailed' from West to East Loch Tarbert, Kintyre became one of the Western Isles. But this specious reasoning no longer holds good, and although Kintyre does its best to exude an island atmosphere it is still part of the mainland.

An excellent road heads southwards, again with a surprising directness. West Loch Tarbert gradually merges into the sea, and you will have fascinating glimpses of the Inner Hebrides. I recollect a particularly beautiful stretch of shore overlooking Jura. Great beds of sea campions extended almost to the water's edge, and at high tide they seemed veritable flowers of the sea. It was still rather dull, hence the colouring of the scene was somewhat restrained; nevertheless I remember this particular view better than many more dazzling seascapes.

But the view was not confined to Jura. I looked across slate-coloured waters to the distant hills of Islay. The Isle of Gigha was quite near, its long, flat coastline reminiscent of some strange basking monster. Gigha is celebrated for its mild climate, its caves and a ruined thirteenth century church. There are even palm trees.

As I travelled farther south I could see the islet of Cara some three miles away. It was a curiously peaceful scene, not in the least rugged or grand, but strangely satisfying. The corn was stacked in sheaves down to the shore. There were no great cliffs and the fields sloped gently to the sea, forming a pleasing foreground to the distant hills of Islay. If this should be your first introduction to the Hebrides you will feel a tinge of that wistful magic which will haunt us more and more as we visit the Inner Hebrides.

Machrihanish is on the west of Kintyre and Campbeltown on the east. The former is famous for its breezy golf links along Machrihanish Bay. A road connects the two places, but once there was a railway—the only one on this remote peninsula. Now that it has gone, I often wish that I could have seen it. I wonder if anything is left of this forgotten railway, and whether ghost trains haunt its shadowy tracks!

Once when staying at Campbeltown I drove to Southend on the south coast of Kintyre. Southend is an odd-sounding name to find in such a remote corner of Scotland, yet situated at the south end of Kintyre it is singularly appropriate. St. Columba is believed to have first set foot on the mainland of Scotland at Southend, although this may have been before his mission to Iona.

I continued to Keil Point and looked across to the cliffs of Donegal on the Irish coast thirteen miles away. It was a calm, still evening with the sunset hidden behind the great cliffs leading to the Mull of Kintyre. The lighthouse cannot be seen from Keil as it is situated to the north of the Mull on the west coast of Kintyre. It is approached by a narrow road, little more than a cart track, with steep gradients, an atrocious surface, and many severe bends. During its course the road climbs to a height of nearly 1200 feet with a breath-taking zigzag descent to the Mull lighthouse. This descent is not far short of 1000 feet in just over a mile. Although this can hardly be described as a touring route for cars, it would make a wonderful day excursion from Southend or Campbeltown. A car could be taken without difficulty to Carskey, west of Keil, and the remainder of the journey undertaken on foot, making a return walk of eleven miles. But given time the road is just passable for cars.

When recently rounding the Mull, I had fine views of this redoubtable mountain road, and if you had ever seen the precipitous descent to the lighthouse you will think twice before taking your car on such a route. It looks particularly adventuresome from the sea. Even the lighthouse appears in imminent danger of sliding off the cliff.

There is much to see around this southern tip of Kintyre. Sanda, a rocky islet with a pier and lighthouse, is visible from Southend, and you will recognise Ailsa Craig about twenty miles distant. There are many caves on this rocky coast, some to the west of Cnoc Moy being festooned with stalactites. The Rope Cave is hereabouts, and a car can be taken as far as Glen Breakerie, which would make a highly adventurous day trip. Davaar Island, conspicuously situated in Campbeltown Loch, can be reached dryshod at low water. There is a remarkable painting of the Crucifixion on a wall in a cave to the east of the island.

I remember trying to get to sleep one noisy night at Campbeltown. My room overlooked the promenade, and Campbeltown was in merry mood. Apart from harbour noises, the entire population seemed bent on community singing, chattering and shouting, and the whole, mingled with odd bursts of music from some undisclosed source, formed a noisy nocturne which I began to enjoy. Eventually I must have fallen asleep, because I awakened to the sound of ships' bells, sirens, hooters and winches, and the plaintive cry of seagulls. It was a gorgeous day, mild and sunny, sparkling and bright, and my thoughts were of peaceful things.

I walked up the Main Street to see the fine Celtic Cross, and then set forth northwards. Davaar Island, for all the world like some strange black monster basking on a silver sea, looked as if it might sink at any moment. I came to a small whitewashed farm near Ardnacross Bay. The corn lay in golden profusion, and there was a heavenly view across to the distant peaks of Arran.

The road northwards to Saddell provided an unending succession of views of the Kintyre coast and Arran. It was a hilly and rather adventurous road. I explored an ancient fort near Ugadale, and later visited the attractively situated twelfth century Saddell Abbey, of which there is now all too little left. There is a holy well near the ruins. Saddell Castle lies to the south-east, and Saddell Glen diverges to the north-west. It was a very hot day, and I came across a group of Highland cattle taking shelter beneath the shade of a tree. They made a fine picture as they gazed in dreamy content.

Leaving the main road near Saddell Church, I visited the beautifully situated fishing village of Carradale, which gave magnificent views of the west coast of Arran, barely three miles across Kilbrennan Sound. The climate is singularly mild in this district, and I stopped by a group of palm trees on the roadside, an unusual sight for the Scottish Highlands. Farther north I came to a little coastal resort rejoicing in the name of Grogport. There is Beer in Devon, Booze in Yorkshire and Grogport in Kintyre. There *is* an inn at Grogport. I walked along the fine sandy beach and looked across to northern Arran. A few children were paddling, and a trio of visitors ate sandwiches on the beach.

Approaching Skipness I could see Garroch Head at the southern extremity of Bute. The road turned inland to Glenrisdell, and climbed over to western Kintyre. I halted near the top and looked back towards Arran, my high viewpoint giving a wonderful impression of the various mountains to the north of the island. This is a most unusual view of Arran, and as you look down the long winding descent to Glenrisdell and across the water to the distant but formidable peaks, you may agree that this is one of the finest views we have yet encountered.

I descended to West Loch Tarbert, rejoined the west coast road, and continued northwards to Tarbert which looked its best in the sunshine. It is here that the famous Loch Fyne herring industry has its headquarters.

On another occasion I drove from Tarbert through the heart of Knapdale, along the adventurous coast road round Kilberry Head.

As I reached West Loch Tarbert, a paddle-steamer was ploughing its untidy way down the loch, probably en route for Islay. I followed a rather lovely wooded lane on the north shore of the loch. Progress was slow but the scenery was delightful. I recall one particularly lovely scene near Dunmore, where a tree by the lochside, surrounded by irises, kept guard over a row of fishing nets hung up to dry.

Time did not permit my visiting the grave of Diarmid, near Dunmore, and the Fort of the Black Dog, but those interested in antiquities should make a point of visiting these memory-haunted spots.

The road beyond Dunmore climbed over a promontory terminating at Ardpatrick Point. I could now see the mountains of Arran beyond the Knapdale hills, with the golden sands of West Loch Tarbert in the foreground. The west coast led southwards to the distant Mull of Kintyre, and the island of Gigha floated delicately in a pool of dazzling silvery light. The view northwest to the hills of Islay and the mountains of Jura attracted me most. The road followed a winding course surrounded by golden brown turf, and seemed to disappear into the incredibly blue waters of the Sound of Jura. The purple, cloud-clapped hills of Islay on the horizon completed the charming picture.

The road descended towards Loch Stornoway, and the Paps of Jura came into sight. These noble bens dipped their purple heights into creamy clouds in colourful competition with the brilliant blue of the sea. The narrow, lumpy but slightly tarred lane descended to Kilberry, and I remember seeing a lone palm tree in triumphant isolation.

There was once a monastery at Kilberry, and the fish-ponds are still to be seen. There are also a number of standing stones and a Celtic cross near Loch Stornoway. Kilberry is little more than a hamlet. The fine white-washed rose-covered post office is but one of several attractive houses. But it was the extraordinary cleanliness of the place which impressed me most. Every stone looked as if it had been scrupulously scrubbed and polished. I was lucky to see the children coming out from school. It was a revelation. You might expect this remote hamlet to harbour a poorly-clad indigent people with unkempt, despondent children. Nothing of the sort. I have rarely seen cleaner, tidier or better-looking children. They were well-behaved and watched me with a polite interest as they chatted together in groups before going home. I watched two little girls set forth side by side along the road towards Ardpatrick. They were in a little world of their own; a world of peaceful, happy, sunny days; a world of colour and beauty such as we of an older generation rarely know, and are less likely to know in a civilisation which seeks destruction rather than the beautiful things of life.

A depressing feature of Scottish travel is the fact that you must leave so many interesting places just when you have grown to like them. This is especially true of Knapdale, a district small in area but full of good things. The road from Kilberry to Ormsary is an example. Hardly a mile passes without its quota of new and increasingly splendid scenery. The Paps of Jura, seen from Kilberry Head, achieve an almost unreal beauty of form. Distance appears meaningless, and these splendid peaks seem to float on the ocean like a mirage.

Other matters began to occupy my attention, as the road narrowed to such an extent that I thought it would expire at any moment. The surface was grass-grown in the centre, but narrow strips of tar still persisted on either side. Progress was slow and bumpy, and I began to feel like a cork on a rough sea.

The road crept down to the water's edge, and followed the shores of Loch Caolisport to the captivating little hamlet of Ormsary, one of the lesser known gems of Knapdale. A herd of serious looking cattle lay stretched on the white sands of the beach under an almost tropical sun. One cow, with a pair of enormous horns, sat indifferent to the playful attentions of the incoming tide just as if she were a bovine Canute.

Loch Caolisport became increasingly lovely, and I stopped to feast my eyes upon a field of corn whose golden sheaves lay in colourful profusion by the lochside. The richly wooded hills beyond Ellary on the far side of the loch looked most inviting. I was directly opposite an ancient ruined chapel and St. Columba's Cave, where the saint is said to have stayed on his way to Iona in 563. There is a rough track from South Knapdale to Kilmory and Ellary, but I doubt whether this route is practicable for cars. Kilmory is more easily reached from North Knapdale on the shores of Loch Sween. There are some very fine sculptured Celtic monuments in Kilmory Chapel, including the Macmillan Cross. The ruins of Castle Sween stand some three miles to the north.

I turned towards brown bracken-covered hills, and began a long winding ascent across the backbone of Knapdale. From the top I looked back into this strangely beautiful land. The road wound in long sinuous curves down to South Knapdale and Loch Caolisport. I could see the rugged outline of the Point of Knap, and beyond the Sound of Jura a faint line of cumulus clouds capped the remote heights of Islay. There were familiar views from the long descent to Loch Fyne. Lochgilphead, although several miles distant, seemed quite near, and the lofty hills of Cowal melted into the great peaks of Northern Argyll.

On another warm sunny morning I left Lochgilphead and drove across the Great Moss or Moine Mhor, passing within a couple of miles of the hill of Dunadd, the seat of the kings of Dalriada who originally came over from Ireland. The footprint of Dunadd is carved out of the rock near the top of the hill, and there is also the figure of a wild boar. The first of the kings of Dalriada is said to have stood here on his coronation day.

My course lay southwards, and I crossed the Crinan Canal and came to Bellanoch, a pretty little place. The canal is very narrow here, and beside the bridge a little garden full of rich red roses and tall sweet peas made a welcome patch of colour. I watched a rusty-nosed steamer cautiously picking its way round the bends of this river-like canal.

The story of the Crinan Canal is interesting, Although begun in 1793 it was not cut until 1801, being finally completed in 1817. Horse-drawn barges were used at first, and Queen Victoria described her visit in her Highland journal. She rode a lavishly decorated barge drawn by three horses mounted by postillions dressed in scarlet. If only I had been there with my camera!

The canal is now little-used. Although covering only nine miles during its curious course from Ardrishaig to Crinan, there are no less than fifteen locks, nine of them in one mile.

Many Scottish hotels are built with an eye to the surrounding views, and the one at Crinan is an excellent example of this highly commendable practice. It is a massive place built on a rocky promontory overlooking Duntroon Castle, less than a mile across the broad waters of Crinan Loch. There are fine seascapes to be viewed from Crinan. You can look across the Sound of Jura to northern Jura and the Isle of Scarba. The Dorus Mor, near Craignish Point, has fierce tidal currents, and it was here that the *Comet* was wrecked. But the whirlpool of Corrievreckan, several miles to the north-west between Scarba and Jura, is much more spectacular, as we shall see in a later chapter.

There are many interesting stories of Duntroon Castle, especially the one describing how Colla Ciotach, before attacking the castle, sent his piper to investigate. He secured admission, but was suspected and imprisoned in a turret, from where he played a warning on his pipes to his master who was approaching with his galleys. The player was killed and buried in the castle, which is said to be haunted by his ghost.

I found it difficult to tear myself away from the wall between drive and sea at the Crinan Hotel. It was just like looking from the deck of a ship across cool blue waters, and it was hard to believe that I was not at sea.

The attractions of Loch Sween are far famed. The road descends to the water's edge, and I quickly became aware of the rich beauty of this sheltered loch. It was here that I overtook a brake, complete with top-hatted driver, galloping merrily towards Tayvallich.

The tide was out, and the strong tang of seaweed filled the air. There were several small boats on the still waters of the loch as I came to sleepy Tayvallich. I may have arrived at a period of midday siesta, or the place may be always like this, but a dreamy spell was cast on Tayvallich from which I found it difficult to escape. There was a boat containing a small boy, who was resting in an attitude of supreme content. Here and there, dotted about the landscape, were other people in similar posture. I lit a cigarette and began to wonder whether there was any real reason why I should not absorb this sleepy content. There seemed no hurry. The sun beat down upon the dazzling blue waters of the loch, and little flickers of heat were rising from the road just ahead. I began to feel sleepy. The boy in the boat opposite was nearly asleep. Scarcely a sound broke the stillness of day. Conversation in Tayvallich must be carried on in a hushed whisper. Time was the only rapid mover in this slumbering world, and of this I was made acutely aware by the car clock. With a great effort I decided that this sort of thing must cease, so I started the engine and turned the car round. The little boy looked up reproachfully, as if I had disturbed his siesta and broken the peace of the afternoon.

The winding route back to Bellanoch kept me busy, and so effectively broke the spell of Tayvallich that, by the time I had rejoined the Crinan Canal nothing remained of my erstwhile feeling of rest. I made a mental note, however, that as an antidote for the tumult of modern civilisation, Tayvallich must reign supreme.

Again passing the sweet-scented roses and colourful sweet peas at Bellanoch, my route led eastwards, and kept close to the Crinan Canal, whose many locks became evident. A small steamer just about fills one of these locks, and, bulging out in every direction, gives the impression of an angry hen perched on a small nest.

I turned northwards at Cairnbaan, and traversed another lonely expanse of the Great Moss. All this district is rich in prehistoric remains. I have already mentioned the Hill of Dunadd, but there are also many standing stones in the neighbourhood, some of which are said to have been quarried from a hill near Kilmichael, or Glassary as it used to be called. Standing stones sometimes, but not always, denoted burial places, and monoliths can be seen near the burial cairns at Nether Largie, to the south of Kilmartin. There are many other cairns and cup-and-ring marks in this neighbourhood, and I know of no other district in Scotland richer in archaeological treasures.

eraray, showing
e castle and
niquoich

ARGYLL

Loch Awe at
Portinisherrich

Loch Awe and
Ardchonell Cas

ARGYLL

Clachan Bri
" The bridge
the Atlantic "

Apart from the neolithic remains, there are many other important relics of the past, including several Celtic sculptured slabs and crosses in the churchyard at Kilmartin. The most interesting of these is a broken cross-shaft to the right of the path through the churchyard as you enter by the gate. The representation of Christ is beautifully carved. The whole effect is poignant, and, despite its great age (probably a thousand years at least), the carving is in a fair state of preservation.

Just over a mile to the north of Kilmartin I came to the gaunt and forbidding ruins of Carnassarie Castle, crowning a hill to the left of the road. This was built in the sixteenth century by 'The Big Carswell of Carnasserie'. Loch Craignish is seen from the descent to Salachary, and the view extends to Scarba and Jura. The long peninsula culminating at Craignish Point prevents any glimpse of the Strait of Corrievreckan, but in clear weather Craignish Point provides a distant view of the Whirlpool of Corrievreckan.

I reached the sea again at Asknish, with its intriguing views across to the isles of Shuna and Luing. Then followed several miles of coastal road. The new road has been built high above the old Pass of Melfort, and gives a most beautiful view of Loch Melfort. The old pass can only be explored on foot, and if you want a glimpse of absolutely unspoiled scenery I cannot over-emphasise the beauty of this short walk. The road is now little more than a path, and is cut in places along the face of a cliff overhanging a richly-wooded gorge. The River Oude follows a tumultuous course far below. I followed this delightful sylvan walk, and, apart from disturbing a few surprised sheep and rabbits, enjoyed complete solitude.

There is something rather sad about following a forgotten highway. It can be a ghostly experience, haunted by the past. But as I strolled along this mossy path, sometimes crackling a fallen twig—an appropriate sound set against the chatter of distant, falling water—my thoughts were far from sad. The sun shone through the trees and flooded the ferns and bracken with golden light. The scene only lacked fairies lurking in the deep, cool shadows.

I came to Kilninver, followed the captivating shores of Loch Feochan with its rich fringes of saffron-coloured seaweed, climbed a hill and descended into Oban.

CHAPTER SIX

OBAN TO LOCH AWE AND GLENCOE

OBAN has been called the 'Charing Cross of the Highlands', and it is certainly one of the best touring centres in Scotland. It is set around a landlocked bay, surrounded by wooded hills giving widespread views over the Firth of Lorne and Mull, and is sheltered from the sea by the Isle of Kerrera. The town is clean, bright and captivating, with a mild climate, good shops and many fine villas on the surrounding hills. Few resorts are better equipped with well-situated hotels and boarding-houses.

Oban is dominated by the McCaig Tower, a circular Colosseum surmounting a hill overlooking the town. It is an architectural feature liked by some and equally disliked by others. One can at least say that it gives Oban individuality. Pulpit Hill is a superb viewpoint to the south of the town, from which, apart from the glorious seaward views of the Sound of Mull and Firth of Lorne, there is an impressive inland view to Ben Cruachan. The town itself is directly beneath, and you will never see Oban from a more perfect viewpoint. I like best to come here at sunset and look across Kerrera to the Sound of Mull, shimmering in golden light and set between the bold outline of the mountains of Mull and the lonely hills of Morven. On the far horizon, beyond this glittering gateway, I try to visualise the mystic realm of Tir-nan-Og, Land of the Ever Young. Under such conditions and from such a vantage point the call of the Hebrides is well nigh irresistible.

I cannot speak too highly of Oban as a touring centre. Despite the wide variety of motor tours, you will find that some of the best excursions are by sea. If you have no car the railway penetrates fascinating country, some of it unapproachable by road. There are excellent bus services and a wealth of motor coach trips. Sometimes, as I shall relate, road, rail and sea trips can be combined.

You will enjoy a brisk walk along the Corran Esplanade to Dunollie Castle and Ganavan Sands. There is not much left of the castle, ancient

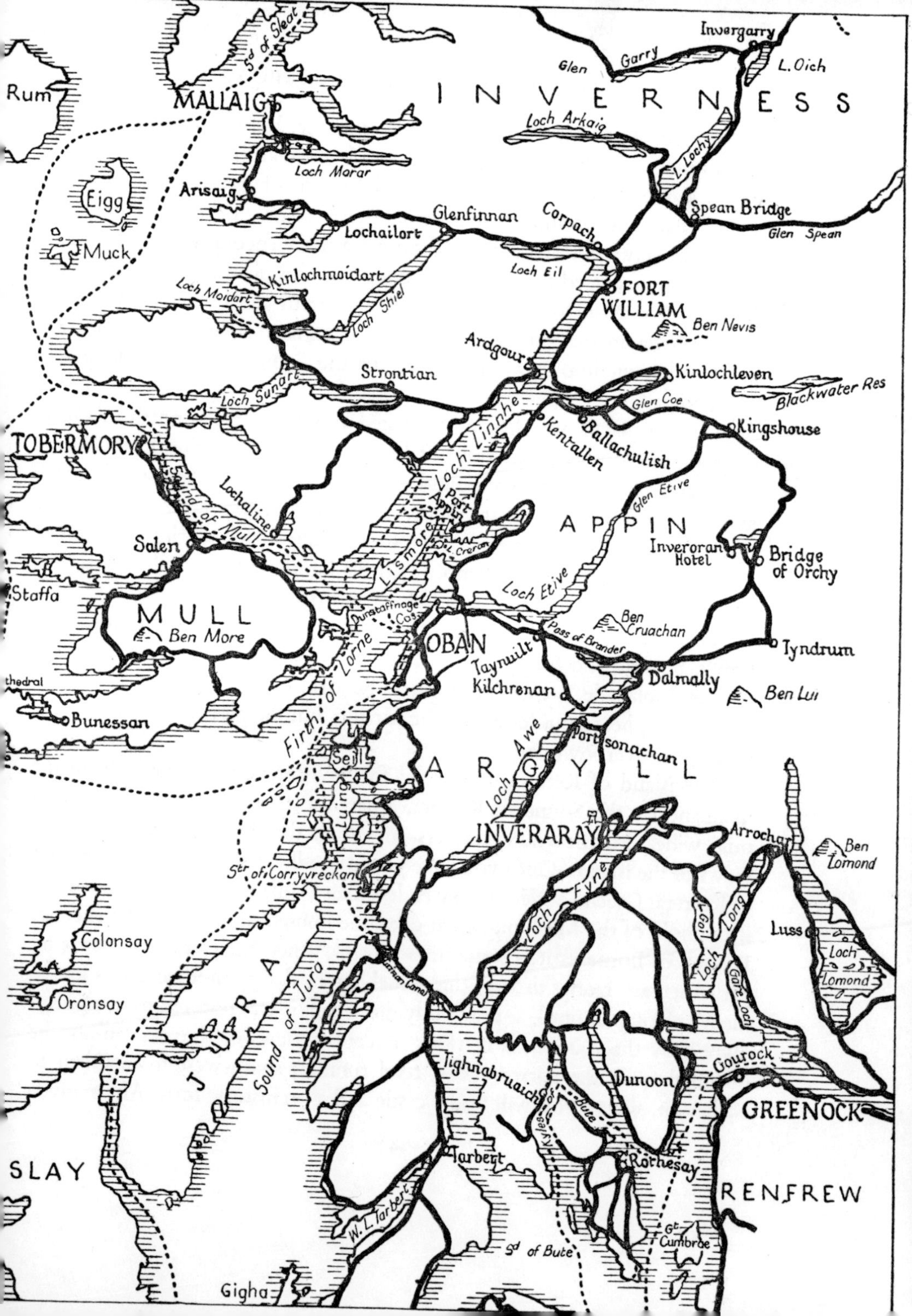

Rum
MALLAIG
Sd of Sleat
Invergarry
Glen Garry
L. Oich
INVERNESS
Loch Arkaig
L. Lochy
Loch Morar
Arisaig
Eigg
Muck
Lochailort
Glenfinnan
Corpach
Spean Bridge
Glen Spean
Loch Eil
Kinlochmoidart
Loch Moidart
Loch Shiel
FORT WILLIAM
Ben Nevis
Ardgour
Strontian
Kinlochleven
Blackwater Res
Loch Sunart
Glen Coe
Kingshouse
TOBERMORY
Kentallen
Ballachulish
Loch Linnhe
Sound of Mull
Lochaline
Port Appin
Glen Etive
APPIN
Lismore
L. Creran
Salen
Inveroran Hotel
Bridge of Orchy
Staffa
Loch Etive
MULL
Dunstaffnage Cas.
Ben Cruachan
Ben More
Pass of Brander
OBAN
Taynuilt
Tyndrum
thedral
Firth of Lorne
Dalmally
Kilchrenan
Ben Lui
Bunessan
Port Sonachan
Seil
ARGYLL
Loch Awe
Luing
INVERARAY
Arrochar
Ben Lomond
Str of Corryvreckan
Loch Fyne
L. Goil
Loch Long
Luss
Colonsay
Crinan Canal
Loch Lomond
Oronsay
JURA
Gare Loch
Sound of Jura
Tighnabruaich
Gourock
Dunoon
Kyles of Bute
GREENOCK
SLAY
Tarbert
Rothesay
RENFREW
W. L. Tarbert
Gt Cumbrae
Sd of Bute
Gigha

stronghold of the MacDougalls, Lords of Lorne, but its ivy-coloured keep is a distinctive landmark. The key can be obtained at the mansion at the foot of the castle, where also the celebrated Brooch of Bruce may be seen, a superb example of medieval Scottish silver work. Bruce and the Mac-Dougalls were sworn enemies, and during a fierce encounter near Tyndrum Bruce only managed to escape by parting with his plaid bearing the famous brooch. The MacDougalls kept the brooch until its mysterious disappearance at Gylen in 1647, and it was not seen again until it came to light in 1823 at a London auction. It was then given by the Campbells to MacDougall of MacDougall.

Ganavan Sands are pleasantly situated about two miles north of Oban, opposite the southern extremity of Lismore. In fine weather in the season these sands are Oban's playground. The bathing is excellent, the beach is extensive and the crowds are dense. Nevertheless, the scene can never be trite, due to the magnificence of the surroundings—the sparkling waters of the Firth of Lorne, green Lismore with its lighthouse, the hills of Morven and the mountains of Mull, Benderloch and Appin.

There are frequent dances at Oban and you can also enjoy golf, tennis, bowls, boating and fishing. But I like best to watch the pipe bands on the Corran Esplanade, a most appropriate Scottish outdoor picture. The skirl of the pipes, heard outdoors, is quite stirring, but the pipes heard indoors are more than overpowering.

The island of Kerrera, renowned for its lobsters, is separated from the mainland by the Sound of Kerrera, a narrow strait in places barely half a mile wide. MacBrayne's steamers sail down the Sound, giving excellent views of the island. Once you have passed Rudha Seanach, the southern tip of Kerrera, Gylen Castle can be seen less than a mile due north. This former stronghold of the MacDougalls at one time housed the Brooch of Bruce, or Brooch of Lorne as it is sometimes called. When the castle was burnt by parliamentary troops in 1647 this valuable relic disappeared, and was lost to the MacDougalls until, as previously described, it was restored to its rightful owners by the Campbells in 1823. Excellent views of Kerrera can also be obtained from the narrow coast road running south-west from Oban to Gallanach, where you will find a castle and a prehistoric fort. Although so

Whirlpool of
evreckan, and
a

ARGYLL

ale from the
of Seil

Loch Tulla (autumn)

ARGYLL

Kingshouse Ho Moor of Rann

near Oban, this road gives a marked impression of being in the wilderness, due to the rocky coastline, rugged hills and the fact that Gallanach is a dead end.

Dunstaffnage Castle, about four miles to the north of Oban, occupies a rocky peninsula opposite Ardmucknish Bay near the mouth of Loch Etive. It has been said that the Coronation Stone was at Dunstaffnage Castle for a time before its removal to Scone. This seems doubtful unless the 'Stone of Destiny' was originally brought over from Ireland by the first king of Dalriada, an assumption which several authorities dispute. A more likely explanation is that the stone was quarried near Scone from the local red sandstone which it closely resembles. In any case the castle is said to date from the thirteenth century, so if the Stone ever came to Dunstaffnage it must have been long before the days of the castle. The site of the castle may have been the seat of the Dalriadic government between the sixth and ninth centuries. Following the union of the Scots and the Picts in 843, the stone is said to have been removed to Scone, from where it was undoubtedly taken to Westminster in 1297. From that time until it was removed during the early hours of Christmas morning 1950, the Coronation Stone rested in peace at Westminster Abbey. The subsequent adventures of the Stone, culminating in its restoration at Arbroath and eventual return to Westminster, form one of the most exciting epics in its history. Despite the controversy which inevitably ensued, one cannot but appreciate the skill and resource with which this enterprise was carried out.

Dunstaffnage features in Scott's *The Lord of the Isles*, and Flora Macdonald was imprisoned there in 1746. Today only the shell of the castle remains, but the walls are nine or ten feet thick and in places sixty-six feet high. You can walk along the ramparts to admire the widespread view. On my visit I was much intrigued by a relic of the Armada in the shape of a fine brass cannon taken from Tobermory Bay, perhaps belonging to the galleon which sank there with so much treasure. The inscription on the canon gives the name of its maker, Asuerus Koster of Amsterdam. A nearby chapel is the burial place of the Campbells of Dunstaffnage.

One of the best short excursions from Oban, preferably taken in the evening, is a circular tour visiting Kilmore, Loch Nell, Kilvarie and Connel, an incredibly narrow route for a motor coach. Even with a private car this winding, hilly route calls for more than ordinary care.

Loch Nell, 'The Loch of the Swans', a placid sheet of water with shores pleasantly wooded in places, is strangely lonely considering that it is only four miles from Oban. Although the coach driver will stop to point out the artificial island and the Serpent Mound to the south-west of the loch, it is worth making a special trip to view these strange features at leisure. The island, picturesque with its graceful clump of trees, probably served as a place of refuge in bygone days. The Serpent Mound, a raised gravel bank about a hundred yards long, is quite easy to trace by its serpentine shape. The head of the serpent was originally used as a burial ground, excavations having revealed flint instruments and cinerary urns. It is a moot point whether serpent worship ever existed in Scotland, but there are other so-called serpent mounds at Scallasaig and Cosaig near Glenelg. While standing on the serpent's head I was much impressed by the widespread view of Loch Nell and the bold outline of the peaks of Cruachan, a view which may have held prehistoric significance. There must have been remarkable ongoings here in the remote past; apart from the artificial island and Serpent Mound I discovered a nearby cromlech.

A very fine afternoon trip through lonely country is made daily from Oban to the north-western shore of Loch Awe at Taycreggan, the section of the route beyond Taynuilt coming second only to the Loch Nell road for adventurous bus driving. I took this trip one July afternoon, and was quite captivated by the sylvan charm of Glen Nant and the falls of the River Nant. We pulled up at Kilchrenan, where one of the poorest roads in Scotland branches off to Loch Avich and Kilmelfort; adventurous motorists will be well rewarded! Our journey ended at Taycreggan, where you will find a small hotel, a jetty and little else. The ferry across to Port Sonachan is too small for cars, hence this quiet corner of Loch Awe has an atmosphere of remoteness even more pronounced than that of the opposite shore of the loch.

.   .   .   .

Oban is an excellent base for two outstanding circular tours. The first of these covers the southern shore of Loch Etive and the whole of Loch Awe.

Our first halt is at Connel Bridge across Loch Etive. This impressive cantilever bridge, which shines like silver when catching the rays of the setting sun, is a conspicuous landmark for miles. It is second in unbroken span only to the Forth Bridge. Beneath the bridge are the Falls of Lora. You will look for them in vain at high water, but receding tides pour over a rocky barrier extending much of the way across the loch, and so form the falls, a truly impressive scene at certain tides.

I was much amused, when visiting Taynuilt recently, to see the Nelson Monument, precursor of the one in Trafalgar Square. Nelson's victory was apparently first commemorated in Scotland! While at Taynuilt it is worth visiting the Bonawe Ferry a mile distant on the southern shore of Loch Etive. Bonawe Ferry caters for pedestrians, but no longer accommodates cars, and as you stand on the narrow jetty and dubiously view the whirling, foam-flecked current there would be little inducement to take a car across even if it were possible. The wild view up Loch Etive to the distant mountains of Glencoe and Rannoch covers a district unapproachable by road, although there are several lonely paths leading to the remote glens on the eastern side of the loch, a region we shall see more fully later.

We rejoin the main road and continue to the Bridge of Awe, best seen from the new road bridge. Beyond here road and railway enter the Pass of Brander, beneath the steep slopes of Cruachan. This is a cheerless defile due to the gloomy crags on the far side of the long narrow arm of Loch Awe. The road continues by the loch side, and gives a pleasing glimpse of the Falls of Cruachan, framed by a railway arch. The scenery shortly becomes really beautiful as we approach the widest part of the loch. The road actually overhangs the water in places, and has been built with great engineering skill. It is now one of the most popular touring routes in the Highlands.

The Loch Awe Hotel occupies an enviable position on the eastern arm of the loch, from where the view includes Kilchurn Castle and the Strath of Orchy. After crossing the River Orchy we turn sharply to the right and follow the Inveraray road towards Cladich. Kilchurn Castle, which stands on a peninsula jutting into the loch, is now seen from a closer viewpoint. The ruins of this Campbell stronghold still present an imposing picture.

The frowning slopes of Ben Vourie make a fitting background to this thirteenth century castle with its gaunt square keep.

Beyond Cladich our route follows the southern bank of Loch Awe for quite twenty-five miles, and penetrates some of the loneliest and most exquisite regions in Argyll. The road is narrow, tortuous, and has a lumpy and at times really bad surface, but the drive reveals a scenic paradise.

There is a sublime view from the lawn of the Portsonachan Hotel, about three miles beyond Cladich, where you will see the loch, a jetty, a little boathouse, a few boats drawn upon the shingly beach, woods creeping down to the water's edge, and a panorama of distant mountains. I have seen the loch shimmering gold under an almost tropical sunset. I have seen it in the freshness of early morning, when the wisps of cloud have been stirring uneasily on the mountains. I have known the loch under a spanking breeze with splashing waves and brilliant sun. Best of all I have seen it in the twilight when the bats were squeaking and I could just make out a wooded hill across the loch, from which came sounds of a strange and rather eerie nocturnal life.

Our road continues through fragrant woods, past several fine waterfalls. We come to a memorable view of the ruins of Ardchonell Castle on the small island of Innis Chonell. The walls are for the most part overgrown with creepers and ivy, and the castle rises sheer from the loch in an atmosphere of forlorn and forgotten majesty. Few castles have impressed me more, and you can meditate on this poignant scene until imagination runs riot.

Port-in-Sherrich is a small village overlooking the wooded island of Innis-Shearraich. Stay a while to absorb the haunting beauty of the scene. After passing the bleak-looking ruin of Fincharn Castle, we reach the head of the loch at the secluded village of Ford, not far from the main road to Oban, which we join near Carnassarie Castle.

· · · · ·

From Oban to Glencoe is a magnificent drive. We again visit the Pass of Brander and continue to Dalmally, beyond where a road turns up Glen Orchy. This is a short cut to Bridge of Orchy, but if you are in a hurry you will probably find it quicker to drive round by Tyndrum at the start of the Glencoe road. The Glen Orchy road is very narrow, winding and hilly, but more picturesque. The glen is wooded in places, with fine glimpses of the troubled course of the Orchy, culminating in a view of real splendour at the Falls of Orchy. It is not the height of the falls which impresses one, but rather the stately sweep of the river and the tremendous rocks which form its bed.

The contrast between Glen Orchy road and the Glencoe road is almost ludicrous. One moment the car is creaking and groaning as it bumps out of Glen Orchy, and then there is silence and a feeling that you have just taken off in an aeroplane. The speedometer may show twice or three times the speed, but the velvet-like surface of the road and its much greater width remove all semblance of fast travel.

Enjoy this modern speedway for half a mile, and then turn off at Bridge of Orchy, and follow the old Glencoe road to Loch Tulla.

The old single-spanned Bridge of Orchy is still unchanged, but the road to Loch Tulla is now improved although rather narrow. There are still a number of ancient pine trees guarding the shores of the loch, and these relics of the Caledonian Forest with their gnarled weather-worn branches impart a timeless quality to a scene unchanged for centuries. The old road ends for cars at Victoria Bridge beyond Inveroran. You can no longer drive over the Black Mount, but the walker will find the old road infinitely preferable to the new Glencoe road, and as it climbs to a height of 1449 feet there are much more extensive views.

If you like a quiet and cosy Highland hotel you will not be disappointed with the Inveroran Hotel. I stayed there recently in early autumn, and went for an evening stroll to Victoria Bridge. It was a moonlight night, but the marshy ground near the head of the loch was covered with a blanket of thick white mist. The road descended slightly, and I recollect few more eerie experiences than walking into this ghostly, clinging shroud until all sense of direction was lost and the road became invisible. I was safe with a solid road beneath my feet, but I shuddered to think of the awful fate which would befall any benighted walker crossing the bogs and marshland around Loch Tulla were he trapped by such a mist after dark.

I like to capture new sensations if I can do so without being foolhardy and thus causing trouble to others. So I walked out of the mist, turned off the road, crossed a stretch of marshland, and approached the evil patch of mist from another and less secure angle. I then stopped and listened. Apart from the tinkle of distant water there was no sound. The moon shone high overhead and the outlines of Stob Ghabar and its satellite peaks were quite clear. The milky white mist seemed to exude a fetid, clammy effluvia, and it looked hideous in the moonlight. I certainly captured a new sensation, but it was something primeval and frightening.

We return to civilisation at the Bridge of Orchy and head for Glencoe. Despite the luxury of the fine Glencoe highway, few other roads plunge into such a wild and inhospitable country. The railway is even more adventurous, and leaves the company of the road near Loch Tulla to cross the awful expanse of the Moor of Rannoch with its peat hags, swamps and trackless wastes. After this the line climbs over bleak moors to lonely Loch Treig. Apart from Rannoch Station, approached by a narrow road from the east, there is not the vestige of a road anywhere near the entire route. The Glencoe road gives typical views of the Moor of Rannoch, and any-where between Loch Ba and the Kingshouse Hotel you can look across vast tracts of bog-ridden and loch-strewn moorland. On a day of wind and rain the Moor of Rannoch looks what it is, a hopeless morass. On a fine day the scene is most impressive, with a certain Sahara-like quality.

The view westwards towards Clachlet and Stob Ghabar is a majestic scene. On fine clear evenings the sunset view towards Loch Tulla and the Black Mount is of transcending beauty.

Kingshouse Hotel, like Sligachan Hotel in Skye, is the haunt of the mountaineer, and every traveller should call at least once at this famous inn. It is not on the telephone and is now by-passed by the new road, but a loop of the old road takes you to its whitewashed walls, where you can be sure of a warm welcome. It is not very large, and generally seems full to capacity with climbers, which is as it should be.

We rejoin the Glencoe road within sight of the majestic and perfect proportions of Buchaille Etive Mor, a climbers' paradise, and enter the Pass of Glencoe. The Three Sisters at first dominate the scene, towering above us, formidable and aloof. We reach the gorge and marvel at the magnificent road engineering. Beyond the waterfall we see Aonach Dubh, Ossian's Cave, Loch Triochatan and the frowning ramparts of Aonach Eagach. We turn off the main road at Loch Triochatan and follow the by-road to Clachaig Inn beneath Clachaig Gully. The first ascent of this formidable rock-climb is described by W. H. Murray in his fascinating book *Mountaineering in Scotland*.

The grandeur of Glencoe never palls. The scene is always changing due to lighting and weather conditions, and the magnificence of the mountain scenery cannot be over-rated. There has been much criticism of the new road on aesthetic considerations, but I cannot agree that the road is an eye-sore. Countless tourists can now reach Glencoe who could not otherwise have done so, because the old road was not designed for motor traffic. My only complaint is that the new road offers less attractive views—but much of the old road can still be followed on foot.

The story of the massacre of Glencoe has been told many times so I will merely give the briefest possible account here.

Macdonald of Glencoe had delayed giving his oath of allegiance to the king, and due to a variety of reasons news of his ultimate declaration of allegiance arrived a few days late, and was suppressed in order to provide an excuse for exterminating the clan. In 1692 Campbell of Glen Lyon and some 128 soldiers dwelt with the Macdonalds on some friendly pretext, and then treacherously massacred about forty of the clan, including the chief himself. Many of the survivors fled to the hills, only to perish from the rigours of the February weather. The scene of the massacre is indicated by a notice visible from the road between Clachaig and Glencoe village.

The return to Oban can be made by way of Dalmally or Appin and Benderloch. As our northbound route from Oban will take in Appin and Benderloch it is better to retrace our steps to Dalmally and thus see the majesty of Glencoe from a new angle.

During a recent stay in Oban I took advantage of an ambitious rail, coach and yacht trip visiting Glencoe, Glen Etive and Loch Etive, a route serving as an excellent introduction to Appin and Benderloch. Although I had covered every road in the vicinity many times in the past, I had never previously travelled from Oban to Ballachulish by rail nor sailed down the lonely length of Loch Etive.

As we shall be travelling through Appin by road in a later chapter I will merely emphasise that the rail trip is both tantalising and beguiling: beguiling because of the uninterrupted view across Loch Linnhe to the hills of Morven; tantalising because one flashes past the finest scenes without being able to stop and enjoy them at leisure.

The motorist has the best view crossing Connel Bridge, as the railway line is on the eastern and inland side, but subsequently, with very few exceptions, the railway hugs the waterfront for most of the journey. Beyond Benderloch Station there is quite a good view of the fifteenth-century Barcaldine Castle. Creagan Bridge is another good viewpoint. The best view of the whole trip is just beyond Appin Station, where the line passes very close to Castle Stalker. The great disadvantage of rail and sea travel here becomes apparent. You cannot get out and look around. There were several occasions when I felt like pulling the communication cord, notably beyond Kentallen, where enticing views of the Corran Narrows, and later, Loch Leven and the Pap of Glencoe, beguiled my camera into fruitless activity.

At Ballachulish we were transferred into a waiting bus, and in next to no time we were deposited at Carnach for coffee. Thus fortified we were ready for Glencoe. There was little new I expected to notice on the route, having travelled it many times in the past, but the driver was able to point out to me an interesting aspect of the old military road from Altnafeadh to Kinlochleven. This hill-track, known as the Devil's Staircase, is only suitable for walkers. Earlier on the journey I was again impressed by Ossian's Cave, high up on the cliffs of Aonach Dubh, sinister and aloof, apparently unattainable, yet—believe it or not—this nasty-looking eyrie has its visitors' book. This, I might add, is one visitors' book which I have *not* signed.

Despite its new surface, the Glen Etive road was quite a contrast to the smooth surface of the Glencoe speedway, and our passengers were distinctly nonplussed as the coach, bulging over the road like an anxious hen over its nest, crept along this narrow ledge of by-way with the tumultous River Etive disconcertingly cascading far below. I persuaded the driver to pull up at Dalness while I photographed the superb view of the Allt Gartain and the sombre panorama towards Lochetivehead. Beyond Dalness the road reverted to the state in which I had first known it—an honest mixture of sand, pot-holes and loose stones. Although it was early July there was none the less an icy wind, fitful cloudbursts and a general air of midwinter. The rains came at Lochetivehead, and we dashed from the bus to the pier where the yacht *Darthula II* was awaiting our arrival. The Buchailles of Etive were almost invisible because of a cloudburst. I hastened into the tiny saloon.

Somewhat fortified by an excellent lunch, I climbed on to the top deck to find a considerable improvement in the weather. A troubled sky and fitful sunlight lent majesty to the scene, and as we headed south-west I was able to study at moderately close quarters some of the loneliest and least visited country in the Highlands.

At first Ben Starav dominated the scene, its huge bulk rising 3541 feet above the loch, but soon, outlined in sunshine and cloud and towering still higher, the peaks of Cruachan came into prominence. The lonely hills of Benderloch were silent guardians to the west. There are no roads fringing the upper reaches of Loch Etive, and the remote glens to the east—Kinglass, Liver and Noe—are among the most inaccessible in Argyll. Occasional crofts and shielings somehow emphasise the feeling of solitude, and I wondered how it was possible to eke out an existence in such an inhospitable though scenically magnificent region.

We chugged along over choppy waters. The cruise barely exceeded two hours, but it seemed longer as I paced the upper deck battling the coldest July wind I have ever known. It was a grand experience, and I was rather sorry as we approached the comparative civilisation of Bonawe and Taynuilt. We had a fine view of the hideous gash in the hillside denoting the Bonawe granite quarries. The wan little ferry hovered uncomfortably to the south of the loch. Soon we had rounded Airds Point and were tying up at Ach-na-Cloich, a tiny haven, surprisingly pretty, sheltered by trees and nestling beneath the discreetly sited railway, along which we were to be swept back to Oban.

CHAPTER SEVEN

NETHER LORNE AND CORRIEVRECKAN

OBAN is the gateway to the Inner Hebrides, an enchanted region mostly accessible only by sea and air. There are exceptions; the car-ferry across to Skye is so short that it only just falls into the category of 'sea voyage'; the island of Seil can be visited by driving across the 'Bridge over the Atlantic'; finally, there are astonishingly good views of the Hebrides from remote parts of the mainland. Skye will be described in a later chapter. Meanwhile, with the proviso that we shall have to do a lot of sailing to get amongst the Inner Hebrides, there is every reason why you should drive to Seil, or travel by motor coach. This trip will give you a good introduction to the delightful islands off the coast of Nether Lorne.

The southbound road is followed to Kilninver by way of colourful Loch Feochan. A hilly road deviates to Clachan Bridge, joining Seil to the mainland and thus crossing the Atlantic, here represented by a narrow channel almost dry at low water, and pervaded by a pungent aroma of seaweed. This humpbacked bridge, with its single span of seventy feet, reaches a height of forty feet above the channel, and was completed from designs by Telford in 1792. It is an extraordinary structure, festooned with flowers and towering high into the sky.

The road ends at Ellenabriech, opposite the island of Easdale, on which is a small village of the same name. Due to slate quarrying activities the whole community is generally referred to as Easdale, including the neat row of whitewashed slate-roofed cottages at Ellenabriech. The Inshaig Park Hotel is a favourite port of call for tea. If you can possibly manage it, be sure to climb the great cliffs overhanging the village. The view from the top, overlooking the Firth of Lorne, Mull, Luing, Lunga, Scarba and the Isles of the Sea, will give you one of the most breath-taking glimpses of the Inner Hebrides visible from the mainland. Scarba, some six miles south of Easdale, is a strange island barely three miles in length, yet rising to a height of 1470 feet with great cliffs to the south overlooking Corrievreckan, a region sufficiently remarkable and exciting to be worth more than passing mention.

You may be lucky enough to be in Oban when MacBrayne's are running their superb Five Lochs Tour visiting the notorious Dorus Mor and the even more terrifying Whirlpool of Corrievreckan, highlights of a day's cruise only surpassed by their Mull, Staffa and Iona trip. These two cruises are quite unsurpassed anywhere in Britain, or anywhere else for that matter, for variety and profusion of outstanding scenery of the most spectacular kind. It is worth spending weeks in Oban for the sake of these two trips alone—just to be sure you take them under ideal weather conditions.

The Whirlpool of Corrievreckan, famed in legend and notorious in reality, can be the most terrifying feature on Scotland's entire western seaboard. The Strait of Corrievreckan is situated between the northern tip of Jura and the island of Scarba. The Whirlpool, to the south-west of the cliffs of Scarba, only comes into operation at certain states of the tide, when the scene, savage enough at the best of times, becomes transformed into a seething cauldron. No skipper will ever take his ship into these perilous waters at such times. The best viewpoint would be from the cliffs of Scarba, in order to gain the necessary height. A distant view can be obtained from Craignish Point within reasonably easy reach of Oban.

Most books on Scotland give only passing mention to this notorious whirlpool. Naturally, nearly everyone gives the place a wide berth when its horrors are unleashed. But, on the principle that someone must know something about it at its worst, I approached the most likely sources with interesting results.

The Whirlpool of Corrievreckan is caused by a series of currents formed by Scarba, Jura and the mainland in conflict with the flood tide which flows westwards through the Gulf, sometimes attaining a rate of eight and a half knots. The floodtide pours out to sea for at least four miles, and is known as the 'Great Race'. A further complication is caused by the bed of the channel between Scarba and Jura, which is very rough and irregular and probably little more than twenty fathoms in depth. At one point a jagged cone of rock called the 'Hag' is said to rise within twelve fathoms of the surface. Just opposite the channel is an underwater cliff of at least 600 feet. We can now picture what happens when the flood-tide hits against this great cliff and is suddenly constricted westwards into a narrow and comparatively shallow channel in the teeth of a westerly gale. An inferno is released, the whirlpool is formed, and the 'Great Race' pours out to sea.

It must be apparent that two conditions are essential to see the whirlpool in a well-developed state: a flood-tide and a westerly gale. The stronger the gale the fiercer the whirlpool. I am told it can attain a depth of thirty feet. An added element of horror is the noise produced by all this chaos. At its worst the whirlpool is said to be audible up to a distance of twenty miles, and to anyone in the immediate vicinity its roar must be dreadful. It is not surprising that ships give the place a wide berth at all times when there is the slightest likelihood of disturbance. I understand that the ebb-tide, which flows in an easterly direction, is not nearly so dangerous, as it flows through the shallow waters into the deep and comparatively sheltered waters of the Sound of Jura, and should there be a following wind conditions would seem still more favourable. One may speculate what happens at ebb-tide should there be an easterly gale, but the result is not likely to be so cataclysmic as at flood-tide with a westerly gale.

I understand that a sailing vessel may have some chance of survival, even under unfavourable conditions, if all hatches are battened down and a course is set for the centre of the Gulf. The current may then carry the ship through to safety, but if it should get caught up in the whirlpool there would seem little hope.

It is only right that a place like this should have its legends. The best known story concerns a Scandinavian prince called Brecan, who fell in love with the daughter of the Lord of the Isles. His prospective father-in-law was not pleased with the match, but said he would give his consent if Brecan could anchor his galley for three days and three nights where the whirlpool would form should there be a flood-tide at the time of a westerly gale. Brecan was naturally perturbed at such a dreadful condition, and returned to his native land to seek counsel. After earnest consultation he was advised to take three ropes, one of wool, one of hemp and one of hair from maidens of spotless virtue. Unfortunately, one of the ladies who contributed a strand of her hair had fallen from grace, and still more unfortunately Brecan was unaware of this. He returned to Corrievreckan and anchored his vessel according to plan. The first night the woollen rope broke, the second night the hempen rope gave way and on the third night a storm of great severity arose and the remaining rope just failed to hold due to the strand of hair from the erring maiden. This parted, weakened the remainder, and Brecan and his boat were swallowed up in the whirlpool. His dog survived the maelstrom and brought his master's body to the Jura shore, where it was buried in a local cave. Poor Brecan perished, but the Gulf still bears his name.

Corrievreckan achieved new fame when it formed the climax to one of the finest films ever to be made of the Scottish scene—*I Know Where I'm Going*—which culminated in a most spectacular whirlpool sequence. Here is the report of Vivienne Knight, former Director of Publicity for Michael Powell and Emeric Pressburger Productions:

The greater part of the magnificent storm sequence in *I Know Where I'm Going* was made in waters that are charted by the British Navy as un-navigable. This location was the famous and dangerous whirlpool of Corrievreckan, which lies between the islands of Scarba and Jura off the Argyllshire coast. The Straits are especially dangerous to small craft; perfect timing and most skilful piloting are needed to use the swell of the sea to carry the boat over the whirlpool, otherwise there is great danger of being smashed against the massive rocks which line the Straits.

Michael Powell and the camera crew made the trip three times in *The Islander*, a three-and-a-half ton thirty-footer which was skippered by her owner, Mr Ian Mackenzie of Iona. Wendy Hiller played some of the most dramatic scenes during the race through Corrievreckan—no small histrionic feat under such conditions. She maintains that only very hot baths and real Highland whisky saved her life after this almost too thrilling location....

Although the Straits of Corrievreckan are uncharted by Naval authorities, we managed, with some difficulty, to take two motor boats through at the right pitch of the tide: one boat carrying the artists and the other the camera. This was naturally a hazardous project, but we succeeded in obtaining all the necessary establishing shots on our first passage through the Straits.

My own attempts to contact Corrievreckan did not materialise until the summer of 1952, when I was able to put into operation various projects which I had long had in mind. In all my researches I had never heard of anyone using Craignish Point as a viewpoint for Corrievreckan, despite the fact that the mainland here approached to within four miles of the Whirlpool, giving an uninterrupted view. The map indicated a fairly high viewpoint, an absolute essential, so to Craignish Point I would go.

I rather suspect that my friends in Oban considered my enthusiasm for Corrievreckan somewhat odd, nevertheless, on a certain sunny morning in June, I sped southwards and was soon following the inviting road round Loch Feochan. It seemed incredible that my car might take me to within sight of Corrievreckan and that I might walk to a still better viewpoint.

The saffron seaweed of Feochan, the blue of the waters and the grandeur of the hills bounded by billowing clouds, a scene typical of Nether Lorne, formed a delightful introduction to a day which promised to be more than usually interesting. There would just be time to make the long detour to Easdale for lunch at the Inshaig Park Hotel, where I might also check up on the state of the tides at Corrievreckan. I left the main road at Kilninver and followed the undulating road to Seil. Profusely sprouting flowers made Clachan Bridge a riot of colour, and I was unable to resist a pause for photography.

There is a lovely view of Easdale just before the road descends to the Seil shore. On this day of crystal clarity I risked a late lunch by climbing the cliffs above the village, my favourite viewpoint in this part of the world. There can be fewer finer outlooks than this, a scene bounded by the mountains of Mull, the Isles of the Sea, and Scarba—aloof and mysterious—hiding the secrets of Corrievreckan. After an excellent lunch the proprietor warned me that I should only just have time to get to Craignish Point if I was to be lucky with the tides.

It did indeed prove a tricky drive, the return to Kilninver and the winding main road south to Kilmelfort and Kintraw compelling leisurely progress. At last I turned along the narrow by-road closely hugging the western shore of Loch Craignish—a most delightful lane by the waterfront—and continued to Craignish Castle, where I crossed the peninsula and quite suddenly came in sight of Scarba, surprisingly near. A grass-grown track led ever southwards to within a mile of Craignish Point. I parked the car near a forlorn little pier west of Aird, and climbed a small hill rising 193 feet above the sea.

There it was! An uninterrupted view of the Strait of Corrievreckan, barely four miles away. Peering through binoculars I could see a sudden change in the placid waters approaching the Strait. It seemed as if there was a sudden wall of choppy waters, tumbling and boiling in strange tumult. Great waves were sweeping over the rocks of Scarba, their foam-flecked crests clearly visible through my glasses. In wild weather on a clear day this viewpoint should yield very promising results, but on this occasion the scene merely induced a feeling of frustration. There was still a good half mile of very rough going to the extreme tip of Craignish Point, and by now the weather had taken a turn for the worse. It was early evening and the glorious clarity was giving way to a dull haze draining away all colour from the scene.

Craignish Point is indeed a journey's end. You could step right off it straight into the Dorus Mor, a notorious tide-race of evil repute. Despite calm weather this was a strangely exciting scene, with capricious currents twisting and turning all over the place, weird eddies and miniature whirl-pools—daughters of Corrievreckan—the whole streaming mass presenting a picture of sullen unease. It was quite a thought to realise I should soon be navigating the Dorus Mor and Corrievreckan itself.

If ever you want to be alone, you stand every chance of success at Craignish Point—a very vulnerable position, I might add, if ever the mermaids of Corrievreckan are out on a foraging expedition.

In the hush of evening I had this strange world to myself. A white yacht crept toylike towards Luing, but I could hear no sound. A pool of mist gathered over Corrievreckan, and a hazy sunset tried to break through over Scarba. Soon the grey of dusk began to settle, and I made my way out of this desolate region and drove back to the comforts of Oban.

There was a good deal of mist and low cloud on the day when I embarked for Corrievreckan, armed with two camera outfits, batteries of lenses, binoculars, maps and various books. The sea was as calm as a pool of rain-water on a still day. Although determined to miss nothing of this fascinating cruise, it was soon evident that I should miss quite a lot, due to floating fog-patches, at first like a sea-fret, later like huge balls of cotton wool skimming the ocean. Hill-tops floated in mid-air like mirages in the desert. Navigation in these perilous waters under such conditions must have been a nightmare.

Occasionally the mists would blow away and strange unearthly pictures came into view, scenes out of this world altogether, magic, Arcadian glimpses. I shall never forget the cool white of the Fladda lighthouse set against the emerald sheen of Scarba and the blue of the sea. Such appearances were transient, due to the floating mists which would suddenly materialise and then disperse like grey ghosts of the sea.

Just off Craignish Point and the Dorus Mor, which I recognised with something like nostalgia, we had to stop completely because of a pool of mist spread like a white carpet over the sea. All was clear up above, and low hills were visible down to a few feet above the water, but the rocks and dangerous currents were completely hidden. We just could not go on, and I feared that the day's programme would be cancelled. The *Lochfyne* hovered about uneasily, but within half an hour the mists dispersed reluctantly into the sky, and a dazzling summer day came into being. I could see my little rock on Craignish Point where I had sat a few days previously, as lonely a spot as anyone could wish, and soon we were navigating the Dorus Mor and heading up Loch Craignish on a round-the-loch trip. I was unable fully to appreciate this, due to anticipation of the next item on our agenda, a trip to the Whirlpool of Corrievreckan.

I found the excitement intense as we rounded Craignish Point and headed for the narrow gap between Scarba and Jura, just four miles away— the same four miles I had found so frustrating when viewed from the land. The mists had left an aftermath of slight haze, but this, too, was dispersing and the view ahead was embellished with evanescent tints of the purest pastel colours, unreal and unearthly, a fitting background for Corrievreckan. We obtained splendid views of Scarba, an island once populated, as the ruins of a church bear witness. I am told that the one inhabited house is occupied by a keeper who, with red deer for company, must have nerves of steel, for I can think of few lonelier or wilder homesteads.

Although the sea was still as liquid glass approaching the Strait, and conditions as calm as could be (otherwise the *Lochfyne* would never have

Plate 28. The charm of Dalness, looking towards the head of Loch Etive

*The Pass of
Glencoe: the go
from the top of
the waterfall*

GLENCOE

been making the voyage), it was soon possible to discern a strangely disconcerting line of water, beyond which all was confusion and chaos. Quite soon we were in amongst it. The *Lochfyne* lurched and swayed unhappily as if well aware that she was in the most dangerous waters in Britain. The great cliffs of Scarba towered menacingly to starboard, and the cruel rocks of Jura closed in to port. I was extremely busy with my camera trying to locate the exact site of the whirlpool, a problem made difficult by the forceful eddies, gyrating currents, semi-circles of water and a continuous popple of wavelets here and there crested with foam. It was as if some inexorable force deep down were pushing the surface of the sea above its true level. Perched on top of the boat deck I could just make out one great loop of water slowly revolving, and this must have been the outline of the whirlpool itself, an outline which would soon be transformed into a roaring cauldron. Although safe enough for large craft under favourable conditions, I cannot visualise a rowing boat at any time surviving for long in the whirlpool area. It would seem impossible to row or swim against such conflicting currents, and I make this observation just in case any enthusiast might utilise apparently favourable weather to row into Corrievreckan from Jura or Craignish.

Scarba is a quite frightening island, barely three miles long and two miles across, yet rising to a height of 1470 feet. To the west of the island great waterfalls thunder down the cliffs and sullen rollers cream over the rocky ledges along the waterfront, an area probably never trodden by man.

Although the rest of the trip came as an anticlimax after Corrievreckan, our cruise proved of absorbing interest. We headed north-west to the lonely Garvellochs, those wild yet lovely isles maintaining eternal guard at the gateway to the Firth of Lorne. Our course lay past the treacherous rocks, to the south of Eileach an Naoimh, sometimes visible as green reefs pouring water from receding waves, and soon afterwards invisible beneath the restless sea. We then bore north-east parallel to the Garvellochs, which, from some aspects, have the appearance of great galleons outward bound.

On Eileach an Naoimh, the Holy Rocks of old, are the remains of the ancient monastery of Ailech, founded by St. Brendan, possibly in 542, relics older than the original settlements on Iona, its close successor. St. Brendan also used A Chuli, a smaller island to the north-east, as a retreat. Dun Chonnuill, at the extreme north-east of the Garvellochs, was an ancient fort of the Dalriadan kings.

St. Columba came to the Garvellochs in 562 on his way to Iona from Kintyre, and most authorities believe Eileach an Naoimh to be the elusive Hinba, an island where he often came for meditation. Adamnan, a seventh century Abbot of Iona and St. Columba's biographer, gives many references to Hinba and its great attraction for the Saint, who was undeterred by the perils of sixth century navigation past the dreaded Torran Rocks off the Ross of Mull. It has been claimed, though without much authority, that St. Columba's mother, Eithne, was laid to rest on Eileach an Naoimh, and her grave marked by a weather-worn stone incised with a cross overlooking Scarba. This stone is still standing.

The existing remains on this ancient and picturesque island of St. Brendan include portions of the original monastery, the chapel, remains of two bee-hive monastic cells, an oratory, and what may have been a cook-house. There is also an ancient burial ground. The whole is now in the custody of the Ministry of Works; admission is free and access is by hired motor boat from Cullipool or Easdale. Needless to say, landings can only be made under suitable weather conditions.

Our course now lay northwards to Loch Spelve in Mull, a sheltered haven dominated by the bold contours of Ben Creach, and approached by a narrow passage between two great headlands. High up on the cliffs a group of children waved to us in welcome, a charming picture on the sky-line. Then back we sailed to the Firth of Lorne, and northwards towards the Lismore lighthouse, seen floating ethereally above a tranquil sea.

Continuing northwards alongside Lismore, we eventually turned into Loch Corry in Morven, a tiny gap in the vast fastness of this lonely region, and the northward limit of our cruise. We rounded Lismore and passed Port Appin on the port bow. Then followed a brief cruise into Loch Creran in Appin, after dramatic glimpses of Castle Stalker against a wild background of Appin peaks surmounted by a range of billowy clouds.

The return to Oban down the Lynn of Lorne gave intriguing glimpses of tiny islets crowded with colonies of seals, who either glared at us ferociously or lumbered heavily into the sea. So ended one of the most fascinating cruises I have ever experienced.

Having run out of film when on board the *Lochfyne*, the final stage of our journey amid the seals was only recorded in my memory, an oversight I endeavoured to rectify a day or two later in company with two friends from Oban. We made an attempt to reach the seal islands by small motor launch. Unfortunately I had not reckoned on the capricious currents of the Firth of Lorne, with the result that waves broke over the bows of the boat and saturated us to the skin. After one large wave had put my pipe out and filled my shoes with salt water, my sole concern was not hunting seals but protecting my cameras from sea water. Our pilot grimly persisted to the bitter end, only to find the seals had departed, except for an odd specimen or two grinning at us from the water. We returned to Oban dripping wet, and so ended my seal hunt with a camera.

CHAPTER EIGHT

MULL, STAFFA AND IONA

IT was 9 a.m. as I stepped over the gangway and boarded the *Lochfyne*, shortly due to make the first voyage of the season to Staffa, Iona and round the island of Mull. I still marvel that so much can be done by one steamer in less than nine hours. The excursion calls for some very tricky navigation, and covers a distance of about 120 miles. You can sit in comfort the entire trip if you wish, and watch the fascinating pattern of the isles pass by. Voyages are not made if the weather is unsuitable, but due to the length of the trip the sudden onset of boisterous weather may have uncomfortable results, particularly off the west coast of Mull.

Somewhat to my disappointment there seemed little chance of this on my early trip. The weather was dull and overcast, and I paced the deck with an anxious eye to the west, hoping to see a break in the clouds. We sailed down the Sound of Kerrera and out into the Firth of Lorne. I could see the 'Bridge across the Atlantic' between Seil and the mainland. I looked across grey seas to the Isles of the Sea, Scarba and Jura. We passed the entrance to Loch Buie, and continued westwards parallel to the Ross of Mull. Colonsay was just visible on the horizon. The *Lochfyne* showed a surprising turn of speed, which lessened as we approached the dreaded Torran Rocks. The sea was very calm, and merely licked lazily at these vicious rocks which lay all around like basking whales. The weather was now clearing, giving a striking view towards the distant Paps of Jura. I thought of R. L. Stevenson's *Kidnapped*; here were the rocks amid which the *Covenant* was wrecked, and we were now heading for Erraid, upon whose inhospitable shores David Balfour was cast. Erraid is the largest of a number of islets, many of which are little more than outcrops of rock. The *Lochfyne* followed a most intricate course, gently drifting between the rocky islets whose seaweed-fringed shores were gently caressed by the quietest of green waves.

The sun was shining as we anchored off Iona, and were landed by boat

*f Glencoe and
Leven from
ur*

ARGYLL

*n nam Bian
Glencoe moun-
from the north*

Ballachulish Fe
and Loch Lever
from North
Ballachulish

ARGYLL—INVERNESS-SHIRE

The Mamore I
from above Lo
Leven

at the little jetty. Our stay was all too short, perhaps due to the fact that this was the first trip of the season. The magic of Iona cannot be swallowed like a pill; it should be slowly absorbed at leisure. The best way to do justice to it is to stay there a day or two and explore the island without the disturbing influence of crowds of hurried sightseers.

I saw Iona on a calm sunny day, with the brilliance of the sun tempered by light clouds. The sands were white, but not dazzling. The water was a mixture of blues and greens, but not glaring. The quiet grey of the cathedral blended with the green of the fields. There was an atmosphere of infinite peace, as if nothing could ever disturb the all-pervading harmony of this sacred isle.

St. Columba came to Iona by way of Kintyre and the Isles of the Sea, and landed with twelve followers at Port a Churiach on 12th May 563. The original monastery was probably built on the site of the present St. Oran's Chapel, the oldest building on the island dating from the sixth century. Some writers incline to the view that the original site was to the north of the present cathedral. According to a legend hardly reconcilable with the character of St. Columba, the monastery could only be built by propitiating the powers of darkness with a human sacrifice, with the result that Oran volunteered to die, and was buried alive. The original monastery was frequently destroyed and as frequently rebuilt, until about 1200 a Benedictine monastery and nunnery were founded. The nunnery is of Norman architecture, and is said to have been built shortly after St. Oran's Chapel. The Cross of Iona, or St. Martin's Cross as it is generally called, dates from the Celtic period, and is probably tenth century. It is fourteen feet high and richly carved with a stone ring intersecting the cross near the top.

St. Mary's Cathedral was founded in the thirteenth century, but there have been considerable subsequent restorations and improvisations. The remains of sixty kings are buried in St. Oran's cemetery near the chapel, and date from the ninth to the eleventh centuries.

You will always remember your first view of the cathedral seen from a nearby hill, the ancient stones of St. Oran's Chapel, the dignity of the cathedral interior and the ruins of the nunnery overrun by a colourful rock garden.

Clouds obscured the sun as we sailed northwards towards Staffa, and a certain amount of deep sea roll became apparent. A fresh breeze added further fuel to the sea, but on the whole we had a fairly calm passage. I went to the bow of the ship, anxious to see Staffa. As I approached the island I became conscious of the strains of Mendelssohn's *Fingal's Cave* Overture running through my mind. I have always been keenly interested in music, and this celebrated tone-poem of Staffa is a work which I have long held in high esteem. I know no other composition which so faithfully translates into music the essential spirit of the Hebrides and Scotland's north-western seaboard. The very soul of the sea is in this music, and the haunting sadness and nostalgic quality of the main theme form an emotional background to the entire overture. The force and majesty of the sea in its wildest moods are painted with an insight which shows how greatly Mendelssohn must have been impressed on his visit to Staffa. As the strange shape of this dramatic island drew nearer I felt that no other music could be more appropriate.

To my great disappointment we did not land at Staffa, but merely paused to glance at this strange, fantastic world, and then moved on. It is strange that Staffa was practically unknown before 1772. Now everybody is familiar with its outline, due to the publicity it has received as one of Britain's great show-places. Its awe-inspiring appearance invites silence and wonder. The perfect symmetry of its basaltic columns and the yawning entrance to Fingal's Cave will quell the noisiest tripper. The appearance of Staffa is enhanced by its queer and sinister neighbours—the Treshnish Isles, Gometra and Ulva. The Treshnish Isles are particularly impressive when seen against the western light. Bac Mor is said to look like a Dutchman's cap, but to my mind it has the appearance of a long brooding aircraft-carrier turned into stone.

Staffa is oval in shape and little more than a mile in length and a quarter of a mile in breadth. The island is now uninhabited, and is honeycombed with caves into which the sea thunders and roars, causing strange and weird sounds, some of which are musical and others terrifying. The four main caves are Fingal's Cave, the Boat Cave, the Clam Shell Cave and Mackinnon's Cave. Fingal's Cave is the most famous, and is 230 feet long and 42 feet wide; the roof is 65 feet above the water at mean tide, at which time the water is about 25 feet in depth. The sound of the sea in the depths of this cave is suggested by Mendelssohn's Overture, but I can imagine the reality in time of storm must attain the extreme limits of terror.

The Boat Cave, quite near to Fingal's Cave, is clearly visible from the sea. On a lesser scale than its famous neighbour, it is 150 feet in length, about 16 feet high and 12 feet wide. It can only be visited by boat, as its name implies. The Clam Shell Cave takes its name from the basaltic columns which are curved on one side of the cave not unlike the ribs of a Spanish galleon. Mackinnon's Cave can be visited by boat, and is 224 feet in length, 48 feet in breadth and 50 feet high. The services of a guide would seem to be highly desirable for the safe exploration of any of these caves. From the accounts I have read of the horrible noises which occur in these caves in stormy weather, the main consideration would be the state of the sea. A tidal wave would have disastrous consequences.

We sailed northwards towards Treshnish Point. We were now considerably west of Ardnamurchan Point in forbidding but fascinating surroundings. Ulva rose to a height of 1025 feet guarded by its near neighbour, Gometra. The Dutchman's Cap (Bac Mor) looked quite fantastic. So far as I could see, the long line of cliffs completely encircled Bac Mor, and the queer hump in the middle again suggested some nightmare aircraft-carrier. You get the impression that the island might submerge from time to time and reappear in new situations. Lunga, too, is an odd-shaped island.

As we approached Caliach Point more of the Inner Hebrides came into view. Coll and Tiree were visible, and also that strange trio, Rum, Muck and Eigg. As a schoolboy I used to be intrigued with their names. Now I am intrigued with the islands. There was no mistaking Ardnamurchan Point and lighthouse, only approached by a most adventurous track. This westernmost point on Britain's mainland has fine rock scenery. Its exposed situation is notorious for wild weather, and navigators give it a wide berth. There were fine views of the lonely Ardnamurchan coast during the next few miles of the voyage, and I could see Kilchoan and the mighty sweep of Loch Sunart during our course to the Sound of Mull. We passed quite close to the Rudha-nan-Gall lighthouse, and then turned into Tobermory Bay. The best time to enjoy this scene from the sea is on a sunny evening, when the Sound of Mull is a sheet of golden light and the lighthouse sparkles fresh and white against the dark background of the sombre cliffs.

Tobermory enjoys an attractive and sheltered situation. I like the single sweep of buildings along the harbour front against the background of the more elevated houses on the slopes to the rear. I also like the sound of the Mishnish Hotel. Where else but in the Western Highlands would you find a name like Mishnish! The more imposing Western Isles Hotel enjoys a commanding position high above the bay. Tobermory is now quite famous for its treasure hunts, due to the sinking in 1588 of the *Florida*, a Spanish galleon carrying the pay-chest of the Spanish Armada, in Tobermory Bay. Many attempts, some recent, have been made to recover the treasure. But nobody has been very lucky so far; a few coins, silver plate and a number of cannons, one of which is at Dunstaffnage Castle, are all that have yet been salvaged. But hope has not yet died, and the prospect of an unlimited supply of 'pieces of eight' from the treasure chests of the Armada must be as exhilarating as it is elusive.

The weather degenerated as we sailed down the Sound of Mull towards the Firth of Lorne. It was cold and dull and windy, but I kept on deck and was rewarded with a somewhat gloomy view of Glen Aros and Salen Bay. The grim ruins of Ardtornish Castle at the tip of Ardtornish Point, once the headquarters of the Lords of the Isles, are seen to great advantage from the sea. Duart Castle, restored in 1912 by the Chief of the Macleans, is magnificently situated on Duart Point, and its ancient walls built on the solid rock present an outline as imposing and arresting as any in Scotland.

We passed the southern tip of Lismore, and I looked for the inhospitable Lady's Rock upon which was once marooned the wife of a Maclean of Duart. As this is a tidal rock her fate would have been horrible had she not been rescued by local fishermen.

I have rarely enjoyed a day's cruise more, my only regrets being an inadequate stay on Iona and the disappointment of being unable to land on Staffa. I resolved to make the trip again under better conditions, explore Iona more thoroughly, land on Staffa and attempt to photograph the interior of Fingal's Cave. I had never seen any photograph of the furthest reaches of this cave, a region hiding its secrets in considerable gloom, and the attempt seemed a worthy objective. Opportunity did not occur until the summer of 1952, during which period I made the round trip several times in order to gain extra time on Staffa and Iona.

Although I shall always reserve a certain amount of affection for the *Lochfyne*, it must be admitted that the *King George V* is a much finer vessel, larger, more commodious and more comfortable. Ship's broadcasts include a running commentary on the places of interest seen during the voyage, thus you will be duly warned at the precise moment when the 'Bridge Across the Atlantic' comes into view, as well as Ardtornish Castle, Lochaline and many other places. Ship's officers escort you round Staffa and Iona. MacBrayne's make a big effort to cater for large appetites—breakfast, coffee, lunch, afternoon tea and high tea being available for those who can tear themselves away from the upper deck, or the still better vantage point of the boat deck. I look back on these trips with great pleasure, especially my two landings on Staffa.

On the first occasion it seemed doubtful if we should land at all. Despite glassy waters for most of the voyage there was a considerable swell at Staffa, and disembarking into the small landing boats involved some niceties of timing. The boat rose and fell like a lift, prompt action being needed at the apex of the rise. Laggards were left in starfish attitude clinging to the gang-way, whereas a delay in jumping meant catching up on the descending boat with uncomfortable results to all concerned. MacBrayne's advise passengers to wear low-heeled footwear, and with good reason; the walk to Fingal's Cave from the tiny jetty can hardly be considered difficult, but the conse-quences of a slip could be very serious.

I know of no more thrilling island than Staffa. With its construction of columnar basalt surmounted by solid lava, and its underground network of sea caves, the island is a geological phenomenon—bizarre and intensely exciting.

Landings are made near the Clam Shell Cave, where twisted strata are in abundance. The way to Fingal's Cave lies along the tops of exposed shafts of columnar basalt, with vertical cliffs on one side and an exciting tide-race on the other. This narrow sea passage, a miniature strait, separates Staffa from the Herdsman, a quite fantastic islet formed entirely of shafts of rock, packed together like bundles of wood or stacked vertically. A handrail stretches along the base of the sheer cliffs as a security measure, gaps having been filled with cement and steps cut where necessary. The only danger is from getting too near the tide-race; huge rollers enter this narrow channel at great velocity, and are constricted into a veritable wall of water, crystal clear and sparkling, surging by at great speed. The effect is really fascinating, though I do not advise climbing down to the edge as I did to try and photograph one of these waves coming through. I found the experience decidedly stimulating, but there just was not time to get a low level photograph; there was, in fact, barely time to get out of the way at all. I had to rush up the basalt rocks, graded into natural steps, with the utmost speed, only just in time to look back at the sparkling scene, resplendent with colour and movement. Between waves I crept down to the edge to look into the uneasy depths of this narrow channel, descending sheer into a jungle of seaweed—a stirring sight, this, a world of writhing tentacles ever restless, scarlet sea-anemones, whelks and limpets.

I scurried along towards Fingal's Cave to catch up with the rest of the party. Loitering is not encouraged on Staffa, and if you are allowed fifteen minutes on the island you will be lucky. The path climbs high up round the base of the cliffs, and, on turning a corner, the full grandeur of Fingal's Cave comes into view. It seems incredible that the formation can be natural, so perfect are the proportions, so symmetrical and vast. Much has been written about Fingal's Cave, and so often the reality of show-places comes as an anticlimax to the written description—but not so here. On the superb day of my visit the beauty of form was enhanced by a magnificence of colour transforming the scene into a natural treasure-house, scintillating and almost dazzling, more beautiful than words can convey. Whether the effect is derived from sunlight reflected into the cave through the deep channel where the sea burrows far into Staffa, or from multi-coloured lichen or rock formation, is hard to say, but there seems a latent irridescence which comes to light under ideal conditions. The cave is much bigger than it appears from the sea; this vast nave of Neptune's cathedral is quite awe-inspiring. To complete the impression I must emphasise a factor no photograph can convey—the power of sound. Every murmur of the sea, even the faintest ripple, is amplified and echoed into a thousand whispers, every roar of each seething wave resounds like the crash of thunder. The path keeps high above the sea, a mere ledge breaking the vertical wall of the cave, and at its furthest extremity you can lean over and look down on to the steep shelving heap of inhospitable boulders, piled high against the innermost wall of the cave. This uneasy beach, more like a heap of the steepest scree, reverberates to the impact of each thunderous wave as it roars through the cave, a surging mass of bubbling foam, and thousands of water-worn boulders roar in torment as they are eternally moved backwards and forwards, grinding ever deeper into the furthest recesses of Staffa.

On my first visit the tide was too high to get far enough away to show the entrance to Fingal's Cave to the best advantage, there was nothing for it but to come again, and plan every second to the best advantage. So I made the whole trip over again on an equally fine day, and was lucky enough to be landed at low water. By careful planning I landed with the first party, and was the last to leave the island. Once ashore I raced along the tricky terrain between Clam Shell Cave and Fingal's Cave, and crept cautiously seawards as far from the cave entrance as possible to try and get the entire scene within the limits of my wide-angle lens. This took time. The exposed basalt columns were slippery and treacherous, and only by choosing my limpets with care could I be assured of a reasonable foothold. The scene only fitted into my viewfinder when I had retreated to within reach of the sea, very capricious at this point. There was always the feeling that an outsize roller would upset my plans when I had my back turned. By this time the first of the many had caught up from the *King George V*, with the ship's purser in charge. This gentleman took a dim view of my exposed position, and warned me to get back to the path. On this occasion I got my picture!

The next move was to join the crowd, with whom I could cheerfully have dispensed, get into the cave, take up my selected viewpoint near the end of the path, and stay there until everyone had gone and I had the cave to myself. While the crowds were marvelling, I was busy working out where I could best balance without falling in, and at the same time keeping the camera steady enough for a fairly long exposure. The best viewpoint was a little too airy to be comfortable, but when the last of the crowd had gone I set to work in earnest. Marvellous though it may be to be in Fingal's Cave with a crowd, it is immeasurably more impressive to be there completely alone. To see Fingal's Cave in solitude is to gain an experience almost overpowering in its intensity. I nearly came to seeing it for much longer than I had intended. Only the fleetness of my feet enabled me to board the last boat back to the *King George V*, and I fear MacBrayne's viewed my exploits with marked disfavour.

.   .   .   .

Both these trips to Staffa of necessity involved much lengthier visits to Iona, and never was necessity welcomed with greater pleasure. On both occasions I was able to find the necessary solitude for the best camera compositions, by the simple expedient of keeping about ten minutes ahead of the conducted tour of the island. When the crowd moved in I moved on.

Iona would be a pleasant enough place were it completely lacking in religious significance. As it is, charged with historical import and fragrant with a mystical atmosphere, few places have so much to offer the thoughtful visitor.

We received a warm welcome at the jetty, our arrival bringing out the population along with many visitors staying on the island, especially the younger element—bronzed youths and sun-tanned girls. Piles of gear lay in confusion on the jetty, the sands were dazzling white, the sea crystal clear, the children danced around gay and carefree, the little village with its single street basked in the sun—for a brief time we entered Arcady, where time is meaningless. In my case, however, every minute was spent busy with both monochrone and colour photography. The nunnery garden was a riot of flowers. The fifteenth century Maclean's Cross, a thin slab of carved schist ten feet high; St. Martin's Cross, most beautiful of them all; the broken shaft of St. Matthew's Cross—all these made richly satisfying photographs; but St. John's Cross appeared to have vanished. It was there when I visited the island in 1949. Ultimately I learned that it had been blown down and broken by winter gales towards the close of 1951.

I wandered round the exterior of the cathedral, noting the admirable restoration work of the Iona Community, a group formed with the praise-

Stalker and
from Loch
e

ARGYLL

h Linnhe at
lmallie—mist
rain

A lonely cotto
at Ardtoe,
Ardnamurchan

ARGYLL

Sound of Mu.
and Kerrera—
sunset

worthy object of restoring Iona to its former glory. Progress is being made with the reconstruction of the conventual buildings. The refectory has been splendidly rebuilt by the Community, whose leader, the Rev. Dr George Macleod, has watched membership increase steadily until the number now exceeds 7000. These craftsmen and ministers devote some three months of the year towards restoration work on Iona.

The crowds were approaching as I took a final photograph of the tenth century St. Martin's Cross, superb in its mute symbolism. I like the circle built into the cross, representing the sun and signifying the Resurrection. With an appreciative glance at the red sandstone of the Cathedral gleaming in the sunshine, I moved on to St. Oran's Chapel, pausing to admire the eleventh century doorway built by Margaret, Queen of Scotland. There is little in the interior apart from some fine carved slabs, probably Celtic. I then browsed around the Reilig Odhran (Burial Place of the Kings), mute witness of the supreme regard in which Iona was held in far-off days. Here were buried forty-eight Scottish kings, eight Norwegian, four Irish and one French king.

On my next visit to Iona I went straight to the cathedral, where I remained undisturbed and alone for the best part of half an hour before the conducted tour arrived. Far be it from me to detract from the value of conducted tours; on a first visit much useful knowledge can be thus obtained; but on subsequent visits it is so much better to look round by yourself and absorb something of the atmosphere of the places visited, an atmosphere so easily ruffled by crowds of sightseers.

Although polyglot in architecture, there is a satisfying simplicity and solidity about the interior of the cathedral. The choir and chancel date back to the early sixteenth century, but the communion table, fashioned from green Iona marble, is modern. The silver cross is also modern and based on Celtic design. The sacristy door is much weathered through the action of centuries of neglect, and exposure to the elements during the period when the abbey was a forlorn ruin. The sedilia, situated behind the effigy of Abbot Mackenzie, bear witness to the days when the abbey was a Benedictine monastery. A small cage beneath the east window contains a portion of the stone pillow believed to have been used by St. Columba. This was, I noted, a rough heart-shaped stone, obviously of great age and of such weight that its use as a pillow must have been excessively cumbersome and uncomfortable.

I left the cathedral with great regret, and looked back towards the short squat tower, seventy feet high. The medieval clock in the south belfry was barely noticeable. I climbed the hill to the west of the road (much fencing-off appeared to have taken place since I last climbed this eminence) and looked down towards the cathedral, cruciform in outline and harmonising so smoothly with its surroundings. I looked across the Sound of Iona to the Ross of Mull and then north-east to Ben More, a noble sight with bold contours, towering 3169 feet above the sea. Finally my gaze lingered on that tiny speck to the north—the strange and mysterious Isle of Staffa from whose Fingal's Cave one can obtain such a good view of Iona.

. . . .

The island of Mull presents something of a problem to the tourist based on the mainland. Motorists are hardly likely to consider it worth the trouble and expense of shipping their cars across the sea to Mull except for a prolonged stay. There are two alternatives: one is to garage your car at Oban and stay on the island, taking advantage of local coach trips and taxis to explore your surroundings; the other course is to make day trips from Oban, a method calling for somewhat boisterous activity.

I once made a coach trip from Tobermory to Loch Don. It was raining with that savage determination peculiar to the Western Highlands. We passed the entrance to Glen Aros and the ruins of Aros Castle, and sped through Salen to Craignure and on to Torosay Castle, then the charmingly-named Tangle of the Isles Hotel. I had hopes we might reach Duart Castle not more than two miles distant, but our trip terminated at Lochdonhead instead, where the coach promptly turned round and shot us back to Craignure, where we halted at the inn for coffee and biscuits. I walked as far seawards as possible. It was cold, wet, windy and depressing. The tide was flowing briskly and its choppy waters swept over a drab beach sheltering a few forlorn boats which seemed sad and lonely. Only the inn, with its wooded background, looked attractive. The view towards the Firth of

Lorne and the mountains of Argyll was impressive but forbidding. Yet I knew all would be changed on a fine day, the blue waters would sparkle, the boats would look trim and inviting, the white-washed inn would gleam against the green of the trees, and there would be fleecy clouds over the mountains. Mull would be a paradise of mountain and moor, gurgling streams and blue lochs. But it was not so on this occasion, and Dr Johnson would have been confirmed in his opinion that the climate was worse than Skye.

MacBrayne's Iona trip from Oban allowed no time at Tobermory, and neither did the evening trips. There was, however, a weekly opportunity of seeing much of Mull from the island itself. This was made possible by allowing passengers to take the Iona cruise as far as Tobermory, landing them at 10.45 a.m. and calling for them about 7.30 in the evening. This allowed nearly nine hours on Mull, timed to coincide with various coach trips, the most ambitious of these offering some ninety miles of rough roads, visiting the Gribun Rocks, Glen More, Lochbuie and Craignure. All I wanted was a fine Thursday, and in this respect luck came my way.

It was a glorious day, clear and sparkling with fleecy clouds painting the sky. Mull was a picture, and the voyage to Tobermory passed all too quickly. Duart Castle, bold and arresting, dominated the Sound of Mull. Ardtornish Castle, at the tip of Ardtornish Point, made the most of its scant ruins, once a proud possession of the Lord of the Isles. A few moments later we had a brief glimpse of Loch Aline, 'The Lovely Loch', and the village of Lochaline, famed for its fine sand and the fact that a community from St. Kilda was evacuated there.

I was the first to land at Tobermory, and hastened to the small coach due to leave at 11 a.m. I arrived to find it well filled with amiable ladies. My bulk at the best of times is not inconsiderable, but when augmented by camera outfits and equipment it will be appreciated that my efforts to share a bus seat (apparently designed for a couple of small boys) provided one of the highlights of the journey.

It gives pleasure to record that the passengers and driver throughout the long trip made great efforts to contribute to my welfare. Whenever we came to any outstanding scenery the bus was halted for my benefit while I took photographs. In the way of sustenance for the inner man there was a general levy from well filled hampers—coffee, sandwiches, hard-boiled eggs, appetising buns and luscious cakes. In return I was able to supply a spare spool of film to one of my benevolent hostesses.

Our route followed the Sound of Mull down to Glen Aros and Aros Castle, once a seat of the Lord of the Isles but now a gaunt ruin on a headland jutting out into the bay; Aros and Ardtornish have much in common. We halted at Salen and then headed westwards along that wonderful road between Loch na Keal and Ben More of Mull. During the journey the driver pointed out a huge boulder which had crushed a small croft as if it had been an eggshell. Fallen rocks and boulders from the frowning hills rising from the roadside are especially prolific nearing the celebrated Gribun Rocks, great cliffs soaring vertically above the road. The narrow highway creeps between cliffs and sea amid incomparable surroundings. This view of Loch na Keal and the Gribun Rocks must rank as one of the finest I have seen during all my wanderings in the Western Highlands. Yet this scene was nearly equalled by the view of Staffa and the Treshnish Isles seen from the heights of Glen Seilisdeir.

Another scene of great interest was the long, low, green island of Inch Kenneth, which has associations going back to the days of Columcille. In fact St. Kenneth was a disciple and close friend of St. Columba, selecting this lonely but lovely island, east of Staffa and south of Ulva, as a worthy setting for his church. The present ruined chapel is built on the site of St. Kenneth's church, and there are ancient stone slabs in the interior, one of them showing the figure of a mailed warrior. A weather-worn cross guards the exterior. Boswell and Johnson spent a night here, the former decently re-interring scattered bones in the burial ground beneath Johnson's approving gaze. The chapel was in much better condition in Johnson's day, and he describes a Celtic bell on the altar. Inchkenneth Chapel is now in the custody of the Ministry of Works, and admission is free once you can get there. Access is possible by hired motor boat.

We descended to Loch Scridain and Kilfinichen Church, continued to Loch Beg, parted company with the Iona road and plunged into the wilderness of Glen More through the heart of Mull. The rough track had never

from the cliffs
island of

MULL

Tobermory,
Isle of Mull

MULL AND STAFFA

The
King George
seen from the
Isle of Staffa,
showing the tic
race between
" The Herdsm
and Staffa

been intended for motor traffic, and I needed limpet-like qualities to maintain my position on the outer side of my narrow seat. Glen More, with its great brooding peaks, desolate lochs and limitless expanses of barren moorland, is about as cheerless a region as any in Mull, yet it is not without a certain magnificence. The descent of Glen Lussa, with its welcome birches and oaks, increases in beauty all the way. The presence of trees and a cascading mountain stream transformed the scene into a fairy land. Mull is a land of waterfalls, coursing down the valleys, streaming down the hillsides, hurtling from the cliffs—molten silver in the sunshine, windswept and capricious.

The adventurous southbound road from Strathcoil surmounts a wooded hill and then hugs the shore of remote Loch Spelve, golden and sparkling on this lovely afternoon. Then followed Loch Uisg, mellowed by its birch-fringed shores—and journey's end at Lochbuie. The bus was parked on the machair and we were given time to look around.

This little hamlet with its tiny church and the ruined Moy Castle, ancestral home of the Maclaines of Lochbuie, is one of the most lovely places in the islands. Great boulders are strewn on the beach, but the scene is mellowed by the restful green of the machair and the headlands sheltering Loch Buie. An ancient pony track follows the shore westwards to Carsaig Bay, where much of *I Know Where I'm Going* was filmed. The only other route to Carsaig is by a rough road from Loch Scridain to Pennyghael, the one route just passable for cars. The path to the east leads to Moy Castle a short distance away. I noticed that the castle seemed in a fairly good state of repair, though one must admit that as a residence the nearby mansion far exceeds it in comfort.

I made my way along the rocky beach and looked across sparkling seas to distant Colonsay. It was indeed a colourful picture—the contrasting blues of sky and sea, the green machair, grey rocks, brown hills and creamy cumulus clouds. Rarely have I left anywhere with such regret, but then I was seeing Lochbuie under ideal conditions. A south-west gale from Carsaig Bay would tell a very different story.

Lochbuie was the end of the road, and we were obliged to return by the same route to Strathcoil, where we rejoined the Glen More road. This time we turned north-east to Lochdonhead, a sheltered little village nestling by the loch side. Grass Point, at the mouth of Loch Don, is the nearest point on Mull to Oban on the mainland, a distance of barely seven miles. It took me six hours to get from Lochdonhead to Oban—by coach to Tobermory and by sea for the remainder of the journey.

We were only a couple of miles from Duart Castle, but once again my hopes of getting there were frustrated. There was just not time. Moreover the driver maintained that the road to Duart Point was too narrow for motor coach.

The acquisition and subsequent restoration of Duart Castle by the late Sir Fitzroy Maclean, Chief of the Macleans of Duart, is a story worth repeating. The castle dates from the early twelfth century, and was given to the Macleans in 1390 by Donald of Isla, Lord of the Isles. The castle subsequently passed into other hands, and through the centuries became a ruin. After many years the late Sir Fitzroy Maclean, who lived to well over a hundred, achieved his life's ambition by buying back the castle in 1911, and thus after an absence of many generations the clan Maclean came back into possession. A great clan gathering was held in 1912, clan members congregating from all over the world. Sir Fitzroy restored the castle to its present condition, a labour of love carried out with infinite care and good taste. The castle is magnificently situated on the rocky tip of Duart Point and commands widespread views in all directions.

We had tea at the trim little inn at Craignure, cosy and efficient, and then away we went north-west to Salen, keeping high above the Sound of Mull. There were far-flung views of Morven, one of the wildest and loneliest parts of the British mainland, as we shall see in a later chapter. Glen Aros and Aros Castle made a fine picture in the westering sun, the old walls, mellow with age, still reflected a wan life, pale and feeble but still not quite obliterated.

Soon afterwards we descended the steep hill into Tobermory, at least an hour before the boat was due, and I spent the time wandering around, climbing to the finely situated Western Isles Hotel, and strolling round the wooded policies of Aros House. I descended to the beach, which commanded a superb picture of the town, drenched in the evening sunlight and pulsating with colour. Somewhere out in the bay Spanish treasure still lingered, knowledge which somehow added zest to the scene. It will be a great day when salvage operations, which have been in operation off and on for centuries, ultimately succeed.

The *King George V* was the best part of an hour late, but there was still plenty of light on this fine July evening as we sailed down the Sound of Mull. Although nearing 9 p.m., sunlight was still pouring through the saloon ports, adding still further allure to the dining table. I enjoyed an enormous supper. The stewards knew me by this time, and must have deduced that I had walked round Mull.

I came on deck in the cool of the evening just in time to see Duart Castle, bold and upstanding and as unapproachable as ever. It was late when we berthed at Oban, at the end of a perfect day.

CHAPTER NINE

OBAN TO APPIN, MORVEN AND MOIDART

OUR northbound route crosses Connel Bridge, where road and rail are fifty feet above the Falls of Lora. It costs from four to six shillings to cross this bridge by car, but you can walk across for twopence. Nevertheless, if we must pay tolls this one is good value for money. It is a thrilling experience to drive beneath the great girders, but before doing so pause to admire the superb seascape across the Firth of Lorne to Lismore and Mull. I wish there were a few more such bridges placed at strategic points in the West Highlands. They would be a great improvement on some of the small car-ferries we shall have to encounter.

Once across the bridge we are in Benderloch. This is both a district and a railway station, the latter is quite near the hill fort of Beregonium, said to be the 'Selma' of Ossian. As we approach Loch Creran, we catch a glimpse of the fifteenth century Barcaldine Castle. For the next few miles the road keeps near to the loch, until we reach Creagan Bridge. The loch is very narrow at this point, and is spanned by a formidable railway bridge. The road makes a circuit of five and a half miles to reach the point just opposite, but the scenery is worth the journey and there is no intrusive railway. This is a lonely part of the world with very little traffic. The loch is very beautiful, creeping close to the road, which at times is covered by high tides. When necessary a nearby private road is available as an alternative route.

We cross the River Creran at Glasdrum and enter Appin, land of the Stewarts. There are extensive views of the loch on the way to Creagan, where you can look across the railway bridge to the road you left some time before. Farther west the scene from the Appin Hotel at Portnacroish is of transcending beauty.

From here we can make a short digression to Port Appin, less than half a mile from Lismore—a fertile wooded island about nine miles long and one to two miles wide. Lismore can be approached by motor launch from Oban, or by a ferry service from Port Appin, but cars cannot be taken. The island was once the seat of the Bishops of Argyll. Students of Ossian will find the *Book of the Dean of Lismore* of interest. This ancient manuscript contains English and Gaelic poems of great antiquity.

You will be reluctant to leave Port Appin, with its whitewashed houses and fine open prospects, but you may find the gaunt ruins of Castle Stalker even more impressive. This ancient castle, possibly thirteenth century, is built upon a small islet near the mouth of Loch Laich, and is little more than a tall square tower. It gains distinction by its beautiful setting against the background of Lismore and Morven, especially towards sunset, when the surrounding waters of the loch are shimmering with countless pinpoints of light.

The northbound road alongside the shores of Loch Linnhe to Duror and Kentallen gives alluring views of Morven and Ardgour. Kentallen has sad memories, for it was near here that the Appin murder took place, a story almost as well-known as the massacre of Glencoe, and familiar to most of us from R. L. Stevenson's *Kidnapped*.

As we look back to the dark days following the '45, we see that, as a result of their part in that rebellion, the Stewarts of Appin lost their estates, and James Stewart ('James of the Glen') was among the evicted. Campbell of Glenure, known as the 'Red Fox', and an enemy of the Stewarts, was in charge of the evictions. While travelling from Fort William, the Red Fox was murdered near Kentallen by an unseen enemy. Suspicion fell on James of the Glen, and he was taken to Inveraray and tried before a jury of Campbells, found guilty as an accessory to the murder, returned to Appin and hanged on a mound near the present Ballachulish Hotel. I must have read scores of accounts of this murder, and all are agreed that James Stewart was innocent. The murderer was never found, but his name was known to certain members of the Stewart family and handed down from generation to generation. One or two other people are in possession of this secret, but whoever knows may not tell, and there seems little likelihood of solving the mystery. The gun from which the fatal shot was probably fired was found in a tree near Ballachulish about a century ago. Suspicion also fell on the wild and lawless Allan Breck who had been befriended by James of the Glen, but it is known that he was not the murderer. The Appin murder remains unsolved to all but an exclusive minority. So far nobody has sought to include me in that very privileged circle. It must be very uncomfortable to have to keep an ancient and disturbing secret of this nature.

Beyond Kentallen we can look across three miles of water to Ardgour, sixty-five miles away by road, The best approach is to drive round Loch Leven and then take the Corran Ferry to Ardgour. You could save a further twenty miles by using the Ballachulish Ferry, but the road round Loch Leven is well worth while as it gives remarkably fine views of the loch and the lofty heights of the Mamore Forest. On the other hand it is worth crossing the Corran Ferry to save about forty-three miles of adventurous and in places very bad road.

The slate quarries of Ballachulish do not enhance the scene, but to compensate there is a lovely view up Loch Leven towards the Pap of Glencoe. The road to Kinlochleven has been engineered with much ingenuity, in places rising to 200 feet above the loch. As you approach Kinlochleven you may be intrigued by a house far up the hillside on the far side of the loch. This house is reached by a steep drive, and must enjoy a magnificent view of Loch Leven. In contrast Kinlochleven presents a very unlovely appearance, due to the aluminium works. No doubt such industrial works are necessities even in the heart of Highland scenery, but aesthetically they are deplorable. Kinlochleven has a great reputation for rain. Great pipelines connect the turbines with the enormous Blackwater reservoir some four miles to the east, which has one of the biggest dams in Europe.

The road to North Ballachulish keeps close to the loch, giving many glimpses of the Pap of Glencoe. It is a comparatively flat road with none of the high viewpoints encountered on the approach to Kinlochleven. As this earlier portion of our route is directly opposite and a bare half mile away across the loch, it is interesting to stop and trace its outline along the hillside. From this angle the road looks quite spectacular, and seems no more than a cliff path, although in reality it is a singularly solid and substantial main road.

One cold, wet, clammy evening I stopped for the night at the Onich Hotel, on my way to Morven and Moidart. Next morning the clouds hung very low on the hills, and it looked as though heavy weather was ahead. I drove through Onich and looked across Corran Ferry to Ardgour. The prospect was so uninviting that I hesitated, and actually turned back to the Fort William road, only to stop for a lengthy consideration of the situation. Once across Loch Linnhe I should be in the remote regions north-west of the Caledonian Canal, a great natural dividing line nearly severing the north and north-west from the remainder of the country. My objectives were the *Rough Bounds* of Moidart and the remote regions towards Ardnamurchan, where I could expect adventurous roads and scant accommodation.

A flurry of rain smote the sullen currents of Loch Linnhe, and nearly persuaded me to forget about Moidart and continue to the comforts of Fort William.

It was quite an easy crossing, even for my car, which loathes ferries. The water was choppy and uninviting, but I was soon deposited near the Ardgour Hotel. I felt like some lonely explorer viewing hitherto untracked territory.

A narrow tarred road led through a sylvan glade, beautiful even in the rain, and rejoined the lochside at Sallachan. The road then became tortuous, keeping very close to the shore all the way to Inversanda, beyond where I came to a road junction and a signpost bearing the magic inscription 'Loch-aline—24 miles'. It is not often that the more remote Scottish roads are constantly poor for twenty-four miles, but this route was so bad that I found it impossible to average more than eight miles an hour without damaging the car.

I came to Kilmallie, and despite the rain found this a fascinating little hamlet on the loch side, sheltered beneath the frowning slopes of great hills. As the cloudline was still very low the village appeared to be at the foot of a line of dark cliffs. It was a strange sensation driving along this thread of a track, with towering rocky slopes on one side, and on the other the sea.

The road, if it can be called one, turned inland at Kingairloch and climbed to the cloudline. So far I had not met a soul, and as the rain beat down on the car roof and I could see nothing but rain, mud and unspeakable desolation, I began to think rather longingly of Fort William. I reached the Loch Sunart road junction and saw an even worse track leading to Strontian. As

I descended from the clouds to Claggan Bridge the rain increased in force, until a cold trickle of water came through the roof and added to my discomfort. In fine weather Claggan Bridge must be one of the loveliest spots in the west, and even under such adverse conditions it was much preferable to the rocky wilderness I had just left.

I halted high above Lochaline to see an amazing view of Mull through a break in the clouds. For a few seconds it looked as though the sun might shine, but torrential rain soon swept across the island, blotting all before it. I have rarely seen such a strange mixture of unusual lighting. The dark skies, shafts of light and the sweeping cloudburst imparted a rare dramatic quality to the scene. I descended to Lochaline hoping for a kindly reception.

Lochaline must once have been a corner of heaven, but sand and timber were its downfall from a scenic consideration. Timber-felling operations and sand excavation have resulted in a hideous light railway, bearing noisy ugly trucks of sand along to the pier. Tractors, lorries, caterpillars, dredgers and heaps of timber combine with prefabs to turn this pristine fairyland into an industrial nucleus. I will say no more. I am aware that the dazzling white deposits of silica sand help to produce some of the finest optical glass in the world, and as a photographer I should be the last person to complain about this aid to better lenses. I only wish that the sand could have been found elsewhere.

I was directed to a small hotel, and received a hearty welcome and the grim news that food was about the scarcest commodity in Lochaline. At the time of my visit the bare standard ration arrived by sea from Oban at regular intervals, and I was lucky to get a meal.

By very careful study of viewpoints it is still possible to find pleasant prospects from Lochaline. One of the best is the view east down the Sound of Mull with Ardtornish Castle on one side and Duart Castle on the other. The latter is much more distant, but its greater bulk makes it more easily seen.

The next problem was to get to Acharacle, and if the thirty-five miles there were anything like the thirty miles from Ardgour I could expect a very rough journey. The first task was to return all the way to the Strontian road junction.

I drove along the six-foot road, and at length reached the junction of the narrow track to Strontian. I was back in the clouds, and the rain again poured briskly through the roof—something an English thunderstorm had never managed to do. I think the track over the pass to Loch Sunart must be nearly the worst motoring road in Scotland. It might be better in fine weather, but on this occasion it was just a muddy river full of atrocious pot-holes. The next hour accounted for just five miles, but the deluge abated somewhat as I slid down the breakneck descent to Loch Sunart. Nearing Liddesdale I passed a tin shack representing the local school. I have rarely seen a more forlorn or cheerless looking school, and yet its corrugated iron walls could probably tell many a tale of cheerfulness and endurance under conditions which would appal some of our city children.

On reaching the shores of Loch Sunart I was amazed to find a first-class road which could have been negotiated by a double-decker bus. Liddesdale was the limit of the 1939 road reconstruction, and the remainder of the route is first-class all the way to Strontian, Salen and Acharacle. The road from Strontian to Inversanda is similarly excellent, and apart from the bumpy stretch between Inversanda and Ardgour no tourist need fear the Ardgour, Sunart or Moidart roads. But the roads in Morven unless recently improved are only fit for jeeps, tractors and carts.

Strontian is a very beautiful village with a few neat cottages, the imposing Strontian House, boats on the beach, and a lovely green machair very popular with sheep. It is named after the element strontium found in the local lead mines.

Beyond Strontian the road plunged between whin-covered slopes. Never before or since have I seen such a profusion of whin in bloom or such a riot of golden colour. The way to Salen became increasingly beautiful, and now that the road is excellent I can think of few other tourist routes which are so captivating and so little known.

I climbed a hill above Salen and looked westwards towards Ardna-murchan, approached by a notoriously narrow and dangerous road from Salen to Ardnamurchan lighthouse and Sanna Bay, passing Mingarry Castle and Kilchoan. Given a fine clear day and a sturdy car this lonely route to Ardnamurchan Point would make an ideal day excursion from Salen or Acharacle. The return journey from Salen is about fifty exceedingly tough miles, but the inn at Kilchoan would make an excellent base for touring Ardnamurchan. You will find much about this remote district and many other lonely parts of the western seaboard in Alasdair Alpin MacGregor's *Somewhere in Scotland*.

I have seen most of Ardnamurchan from the sea upon several occasions, and have admired the rugged grandeur of Ardnamurchan Point with its lonely lighthouse. As always on such occasions the beauty was there to see, but I had no opportunity to land. Ardnamurchan Point has a terrible reputation for wild weather.

I headed northwards towards the *Rough Bounds*, that fascinating region between Loch Sunart and Loch Hourn, and one of the most difficult touring areas in the whole of Scotland. Roads are few and immense detours have to be made, as every road is a cul-de-sac and the return must be made the same way. Distances by sea are quite short in this neighbourhood, but by car each northward step from loch to loch involves a formidable day's journey.

I deposited my luggage at the Acharacle Hotel overlooking Loch Shiel. This is one of the cosiest hotels it has been my good fortune to visit, and I received a most kindly welcome and one of the oddest suppers I have ever eaten. I see from my notes made on the spot that it included the following: a poached egg floating on a pile of minced beef, potatoes, peas, carrots, cream trifle, cream chocolate cakes, shortbread, wheaten scones, oat cakes, butter, red currant jam and tea. So concluded a rather wonderful day.

I woke early, and anxiously inspected the weather. It was dull and overcast, and rain hung around ready to do its worst. I ate a hearty breakfast, and set forth into 'fairy lands forlorn'. I drove across Kentra Moss to Kentra Bay, where I had a distant view of Rum soaking in the rain. If ever there is bad weather around it seems to fly straight to Rum. But this time there was more rain than Rum could manage, and I saw with some concern that it was blowing in my direction. As there was little wind I counted on a couple of hours grace before the bad weather arrived, so followed the narrow track to its terminus at a little spot rejoicing in the name of Gobsheallach.

Parking the car, I set off on foot to the lost hamlet of Ardtoe. I believe that the correct postal address of this clachan is 'Ardtoe, Acharacle, Ardnamurchan, Argyll'. I followed the winding footpath, and came across an occasional tiny cottage with its corrugated iron roof and untidy sheds. I wondered how anyone could scrape a living from such barren land. But primitive conditions do not appear too great a hardship to those happy people who live in Arcady. Nobody objected to my prowling around with a camera. Little children smiled, and I received a friendly greeting wherever I went. Even the dogs showed no ill will. I seemed to have stumbled on some forgotten happy world where life is hard but worry and care are unknown.

I returned to my magic carpet and drove to Shiel Bridge, subsequently following the Dorlin road to Loch Moidart. This is a short drive through the heart of dense woods penetrated by the River Shiel, whose dark and sinister depths form a sombre foreground to the imposing Shiel Bridge House. The road ended at the equally imposing Dorlin House opposite Eilean Shona and Castle Tioram on Loch Moidart. The bad weather had arrived from Rum, and the rain made the scene oppressive in its dank silence.

The grim Castle Tioram is built on a rocky islet, which can be approached dryshod at low-water by a narrow sand-spit. I crossed the sands at ebb-tide and looked back to the dark and forbidding rocky heights above Dorlin House. Luxuriant trees covered the hills and islets all around in rich splendour. I climbed to the castle and entered through its dark portal.

Castle Tioram was built in the fourteenth century by Amie MacRuari, who married the first Lord of the Isles. From Ranald, her second son, came the Clanranald branch of the MacDonald Clan. The castle was burned in 1715 on instructions from the chief when he set forth to take part in the Jacobite Rising of 1715. The chief feared that he would be killed in battle and rather than have the castle fall into the hands of the Campbells he had it destroyed. But much of the interest still remains. The walls are intact, and the pentangular shape of the castle takes advantage of the rocky outline of the islet. Once you are through the narrow portal you are really inside an ancient castle, and the majestic natural surroundings add to the impressiveness of the scene.

I looked around the courtyard, open to the sky, climbed to the terrace and wandered around the hall, kitchen and keep. This is quite a small castle, and very compact. I crawled into the dank dungeon with its cobwebs and slime, an evil place but superior to many. I have found some so foul that I have passed on, shuddering. I suppose any enthusiast after 'atmosphere' could spend quite a passable night in this particular dungeon, and content himself with tracing the alleged patches of bloodstain commemorating an ancient murder.

I returned to the comparative civilisation of Acharacle. Ardnamurchan was at its best when I set forth on my long journey eastwards—a necessary preliminary to my next long journey westwards. Salen and Strontian looked delightful. I could write much of whitewashed houses, emerald green machair, blue waters and sky, golden whin, fleecy clouds and mountain splendour, but such remarks would apply to so much of the north-western seaboard.

I looked across Loch Sunart to Liddesdale and the hill-track to Lochaline, and even in fine weather this looked a formidable and adventurous route. I had no need to follow it again, and availed myself of the short cut down Glen Tarbert to Inversanda. I had a most impressive view across Loch Linnhe to Ben Vair, but saw none of the stags which I have been told are a familiar feature of this glen.

The road from Inversanda to Ardgour was a sheer joy, and offered unrivalled views of Bidean nam Bian, Argyll's highest peak, and some of the other Glencoe hills. The entire Ben Nevis massif was visible. I returned through the beech avenue, now sparkling in the sun, and came to rest at the Corran Ferry.

I cannot overpraise the beauties of Morven, Moidart and Ardnamurchan and can only urge you to visit these districts yourself, but be sure to arrange accommodation beforehand. Hotels are small and there are very few of them.

I crossed the ferry in company with a Fort William solicitor, and gave him a lift to Fort William. He was surprised to learn that I, too, was a qualified solicitor, and was politely amazed when I told him I had given up law for a photographic and literary career. I almost suspect he was a trifle envious of my choice!

CHAPTER TEN

THE ROAD TO THE ISLES

MANY unkind things have been said about the appearance of Fort William, and I cannot pretend that, as a town, it has the beauty of Oban. At the same time it is a superb touring centre, only comparable with Oban in this respect. Used as a base for day excursions Fort William is perfect. There are many really excellent hotels, good shops, the West Highland Museum and a cinema. There are, too, a great variety of excursions for visitors who have no car.

Ben Nevis is the main attraction for climbers. There are trips up the Great Glen to Inverness. The most picturesque railway trip in Britain runs from Fort William to Mallaig, covering much of the route followed by the Road to the Isles. There are steamer trips to Oban, Iona and Staffa. There is also a circular trip to Glenfinnan. Another magnificent railway journey covers Glen Spean and the lonely route to Loch Treig and the Moor of Rannoch—or you may prefer a combined sea and rail excursion to the Isle of Skye. If you are content to pass through the scenery, and not stop at will, these trips are ideal.

To anyone without a car wishing to see something of the Western Highlands with the minimum of effort, I can suggest nothing better than to stay a week at Oban, followed by a week at Fort William, taking advantage of all available excursions. The excursions will be much more interesting if you have studied the routes beforehand from the many excellent maps and guides available. At the worst, such a series of day trips will do much to pave the way for more leisurely subsequent tours. Once you have seen something of the Western Highlands in fine weather, you will want to go again and again. Very few persons remain unmoved by beautiful scenery, a kindly people and a richly romantic past.

Before we set forth on the Road to the Isles there is much to see quite near to Fort William. Ben Nevis and Glen Nevis are the nearest scenic attractions, but first visit the West Highland Museum in Cameron Square. When I called at the museum in 1949, no illustrated guide-book was available, an omission which should be rectified. You will see many relics of the '45, including the secret portrait of Prince Charles. This is of great interest: it looks like a discarded palette at which nobody would look twice, but when a metal cylinder is placed in a certain position on the palette, the mirror-like surface of the cylinder reveals a charming portrait of Prince Charles Edward. There is an intriguing ingenuity about this relic which speaks poignantly of the '45. Note also the many personal relics of Prince Charles, such as his breeks, a lock of his hair and many letters. The museum also preserves the eighteenth-century oak panelling from the Governor's House which once stood at Fort William. I was particularly impressed by a replica of a croft interior, presented with quite dramatic effect. Many other historical relics are to be seen.

You can get by car to Achintee Farm near the foot of the pony track winding to the summit of Ben Nevis. The going is quite easy, and you should allow about three hours for the ascent and two for the descent. The tremendous precipices forming the north face of the mountain attract rock climbers, but should be admired from a distance by others. The weather is capricious, and there is always some snow on the mountain. There used to be an observatory at the summit, but this was abandoned in 1904. You will find the visitors' books preserved at the West Highland Museum.

There is little hope of seeing Ben Nevis from Fort William. The best view is from Corpach, but there are many other viewpoints from the far side of Loch Linnhe. There is a glimpse from Kiachnish Bridge about half way between Fort William and Corran Ferry. The Spean Bridge road gives many distant views of the north face of the mountain.

You will enjoy the drive up Glen Nevis on a day of exhilarating freshness and clarity, although the road is so overshadowed by the lower slopes of Ben Nevis that the summit is not often visible. This wooded glen gives magnificent mountain prospects dominated by satellite peaks of the Ben Nevis massif to the north, and the mountains of the Mamore Forest to the south.

A good but narrow road leads to Achriach, where a rather fragile-looking bridge, consisting of a row of stout planks across iron supports, crosses a ravine beside an impressive waterfall. The road degenerates beyond here, hence it is advisable to park your car near Polldubh and walk up the glen as far as Steall. The scenery near the head of the glen is of the highest order, but the wildness is tempered by occasional trees, such as mountain ash, and profusion of bracken. The road picks its way between great isolated rocks, polished by glacial action, and there are many glimpses of the torrential course of the Water of Nevis.

There are two routes to the Western Isles—one from Fort William to Mallaig, and the other from either Invergarry or Invermoriston to the Kyle of Lochalsh. Both routes traverse magnificent scenery, but the Mallaig road, in close company with the railway, is perhaps better known and offers greater variety of scene. In fact you will meet with every kind of West Highland scenery on the forty-seven mile journey to Mallaig. There are sea lochs, inland lochs, the open sea, dazzling white sands, mountains, glens, waterfalls, rivers, woods and glorious views of the Isles. The road ends just beyond Mallaig, and cars have to return the same way, unless they are shipped from Mallaig to Skye.

At one time the Mallaig road was a regular source of income to the various garage proprietors of Fort William. The road was in such a shocking state that only the sturdiest cars and most capable drivers could hope to make the double journey without mishap.

During 1938 the road was reconstructed between Arisaig and Lochailort, and now it holds no terrors, although you will still find many acute corners and short, sharp hills. The road is narrow for much of the way, and large cars require careful handling. In any case, the full beauty of this route can only be enjoyed by leisurely progress and frequent halts to enjoy the scenery.

Two miles north of Fort William the Road to the Isles is introduced by a lone signpost bearing the significant word 'Mallaig'. The road crosses Corpach Moss to the Caledonian Canal in one straight swoop, as if anxious to urge us on our way. Corpach is about a mile to the west, and a fine view of Ben Nevis is obtained by walking down to the railway line which, as usual, is at the extreme edge of the shore. Various gates lead across the line to private jetties, and from any of these there is a wonderful view of the ben, with the quaintly picturesque Corpach pier in the foreground.

Once beyond the narrows at Kilmallie the road and railway keep close to Loch Eil. You will pass the old house of Fassifern where Prince Charles took shelter. Still further to the west the head of Loch Eil is reached, and we leave the sea for a while. Except for the seaweed, Loch Eil is rather similar to many remote inland lochs. We pass the junction of the road to Ardgour, beginning its tortuous course to the western side of the Corran Ferry, twenty-one miles distant. Beyond this point the railway parts company with the road, and although it is never far away it is rarely intrusive, and generally manages to hide itself with commendable skill.

Glenfinnan is famous for its memories of the '45, commemorated by Prince Charlie's monument, a tall tower conspicuously situated on the marshland at the head of Loch Shiel and surmounted by a statue of the Prince. I have seen this monument in the drenching rain, a mute symbol of bygone romance and adventure, the sad echo of a lost cause.

It is worth climbing the surrounding hills to the north of Glenfinnan for the superb view of the rugged mountains on either side of the seemingly endless Loch Shiel. This loch has a very straight course for most of its length of about eighteen miles. A small steamer plies from Glenfinnan to Acharacle, thus covering the entire length of the loch. As the loch is rarely more than a mile in width, and penetrates some of the wildest and loneliest scenery, this is a most satisfying trip. There are no roads beside the loch, except for a short stretch between Acharacle and Dalilea in Moidart. About twelve miles down the loch, some two miles east of Dalilea, there is a tiny islet—Eilean Fhionain —where you can see an ancient ruined chapel and burial ground. One of the few surviving Celtic bells in Scotland still remains on the chapel altar. St. Finan, a contemporary of St. Columba, had a cell on the islet, probably on the site of the present chapel. Tradition has it that the saint brought the bell with him from Ireland.

Beyond Glenfinnan the Road to the Isles enters into all its glory, and every mile offers constantly changing views of mountain and heather, tree and loch. Loch Eilt, with its fir-studded islet, has a tranquil beauty which in itself would make the journey worth while. On a recent visit I noticed that

ISLE OF STAFFA, INNER HEBRIDES

several of the stately trees on this islet had been blown down, thus altering a landmark familiar to all who know the road to Mallaig.

There are comfortable hotels all along this route, and I have visited them all. None gave me such a strange sense of living in the past as the inn at Lochailort, where I stayed one wild September night. It was here that I dined by candlelight while listening to the howling of the wind and the flurry of the rain outside. It was here, too, that I discovered an enormous Erard grand piano set in the quaint, cosy lounge, where I drank coffee and ate biscuits beside a peat fire. I smoked a friendly pipe afterwards and read about Prince Charlie by mellow firelight and a flickering paraffin lamp. This inn has an aura of bygone days, and as I tramped along the panelled passages by the light of a guttering candle the past seemed nearer and the present but a memory. In fact the place *feels* haunted, but quite pleasantly so, as if by fairies.

It was different the next morning as I gazed interestedly at the livestock which live round about this inn. I have seen ponies, sheep, cattle, poultry and kittens, and doubtless a longer stay would have been still more revealing. During breakfast, geese and hens were splashing about outside, and a tiny kitten mewed at my table.

The usual quota of guests filled the hotel—climbers, fishermen, tourists and elderly spinsters. The more remote, lonely and inaccessible inns seem to attract elderly spinsters. At first they seem dull, faded and uninteresting, but they often display great erudition and aptitude in accomplishing feats of endurance. The two with whom I had breakfast were cheerfully planning to walk across rain-soaked and bog-strewn hills to Loch Morar. I had pictured them timidly tackling the main road between showers. Instead, they thought nothing of getting soaked to the skin and battling against bogs and mists and lonely mountain traverses.

Continuing our journey we reach the shores of Loch nan Uamh, where Prince Charlie first set foot on the mainland of Scotland. Beyond the sylvan delight of Glen Beasdale we come to restful Arisaig, set on the shores of

Plate 45. The furthermost reaches of Fingal's Cave, Isle of Staffa

Loch nan Cilltean, with its fringe of golden sea-wrack. Beyond Arisaig the road climbs steeply past the church, and soon there is a marvellous view of the far Cuillin of Skye and the Sound of Sleat. The road dips down to the sea by the white sands of Morar. The magic of this place is beyond description. Here you have dazzling white sands, colourful seaweed and rock-pools, while far away, across the blue waters of the Sound of Sleat, are the distant cloud-capped Cuillin. You will never want to go away!

Near Morar, where once were beautiful waterfalls, we can follow a rough road to Bracara on the shores of Loch Morar. This loch is only thirty feet above the sea, less than a quarter of a mile away, but it attains a depth of 1017 feet despite the fact that it is barely a mile wide. Its dreadful depths are said to be inhabited by a monster called Morag, a creature more retiring and elusive than even its colleague in Loch Ness.

As we continue northwards towards Mallaig, the Cuillin come ever nearer, and the strange peaks of Rum and Eigg, distant isles of the sea, become constant companions. You may be lucky enough to see a golden sunset over the Sound of Sleat, and marvel at the strange serrated peaks of the Cuillin as they become silhouetted against a blaze of flame-coloured splendour. Sunsets are always fascinating, and in the hush of evening they seem to induce an exaltation of spirit rarely attainable in any other way. Such scenes are the supreme joy of travel, and their beauty will linger in one's memory through many a dark day.

In the late September of 1949 I found myself at Mallaig with time on my hands. I walked around the cliffs of North Morar to Loch Nevis, the 'Loch of Heaven', and descended to the beach at Mallaigvaig, a tiny clachan in a heavenly situation. There was considerable heat haze, but I could just see across to Inverie Bay and the hills of Knoydart. Access to Inverie is only possible by sea unless you tramp the many miles of rough footpath from Loch Hourn; but it is easily reached from Mallaig by boat. It was delightful to sit on the shore of this quiet bay and enjoy the serene beauty of Loch Nevis. A couple of friendly dogs were paddling ecstatically, and a small boat chugged across to Inverie. You will find peace and dreamy content at Mallaigvaig.

I walked slowly back to Mallaig, descending the steep hill with its festoons of fishing nets hung out to dry, and made my way to the harbour, where I sat on an empty herring box and watched small children fishing. They caught a fine silver herring and threw it into a box, where it struggled to escape, looking like a streak of gleaming silver in its frantic attempts to become free. One of the little girls walked up to it and said, 'It's no use struggling, little fish, you are dead.'

I took another stroll around the harbour after dark, and found it teeming with life. It is quite a rendezvous for the local population, and one or two shops were still open. I noted that a mobile cinema was due to visit Mallaig the following Saturday. There was an abundance of fruit on sale, so I bought some fresh peaches and ate them while sitting on derelict herring boxes. This innocent pursuit seemed to cause considerable amusement among the local fishergirls.

In the summer there are many steamer excursions from Mallaig, including a daily service to Armadale in Skye. Some of the trips are most enjoyable, such as the short cruises to Loch Hourn, Loch Nevis, Loch Moidart, and the Isle of Eigg.

The islands of Canna, Rum, Muck, and Eigg are a strange quartet. I remember them best from a recent cruise on the T.S.S. *Lady Killarney*. We intended to sail to South Uist, but heavy weather was approaching, and a deep sea roll was causing great discomfort to the passengers; so the captain wisely abandoned Lochboisdale, and we turned up the Sound of Rum instead.

We had magnificent views of the Sgurr of Eigg and the towering heights of Sgurr nan Gillean and Askival on the island of Rum. We sailed quite near to these mountains, which rise abruptly from the sea. The dark slopes and frowning cliffs were quite awe-inspiring against the foam-flecked foreground. Rum is privately owned and preserved for deer. Several writers have described the lack of facilities for uninvited visitors, trespassers not being encouraged. On the other hand, Hubert Walker, who took the precaution of first obtaining permission to land, describes an interesting visit to Rum in his book *On Hills of the North*. The island can, however, be seen in all its beauty from various viewpoints on the mainland and from southern Skye and Mull.

The island of Eigg has several unusual attractions, including the famous Sgurr of Eigg. This peculiar hill, a familiar landmark from the sea, is surmounted by a mass of columnar pitchstone with 400-foot cliffs. I should be quite content to view the Sgurr from a distance, but the singing sands of Laig are another matter. The act of walking over these sands is said to produce singing sounds, but some writers who have visited the sands have described the sounds as disappointing squeaks. No doubt certain weather or tidal conditions are better than others.

Eigg had its own massacre in 1577, due to a feud between the Macleods and the Macdonalds. Most of the population of Eigg were suffocated in a cave where they had taken refuge from the Macleods. As they would not surrender, the Macleods lit a fire at the entrance to the cave and the Macdonalds perished hideously. Their skeletons remained for centuries until they were eventually removed, but even today human bones are sometimes found there. Miss E. M. Donaldson in her *Wanderings in the Western Highlands and Islands* gives a graphic account of the massacre, and a most informative description of Eigg itself.

I have only seen Canna from a distance, but have sailed close to the island of Muck. This small island may derive its uninviting name from 'muick' signifying a pig, but it has quite a pleasant appearance with low-lying shores, a rounded hill to the west and several satellite islets. It is a modest little island, and its activities are confined to sheep and dairy produce.

It is always a sad feeling to leave the 'tangle of the isles', but our regret can be tempered by the knowledge that we are only returning eastwards in order to revisit the islands from a more northerly approach.

46

The jetty,
Isle of Iona

IONA

Cathedral:
Abbey Church
t Mary and
'ran's Chapel

47

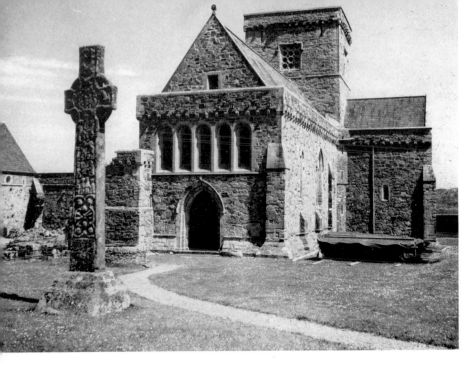

St Martin's (
and Iona Cathec
the Abbey Ch
of St Mary

IONA

Interior of
Cathedral (A
Church of St N
looking toward
choir and chan

CHAPTER ELEVEN

FORT WILLIAM TO KYLE OF LOCHALSH

THE worst plan you can follow on a touring holiday is to visit the most attractive places first. If you do, all subsequent touring ground will come as an anticlimax. Fortunately, Scotland is most beautifully arranged into a series of touring regions becoming increasingly attractive as you approach from south to north. Each district has its high-spots working up to a climax, and as you move gradually northwards the scenery becomes more and more fascinating. When you have reached the farthest limits of the far north-west, then it is time to return home in a hurry before the anticlimax sets in. No single holiday can possibly cover the western seaboard at one attempt. I am just getting to know it now, after more than twenty years of repeated visits.

The more northerly route to the Isles by way of Glen Garry or Glen Moriston can easily be covered in a day from Fort William, but a full day could be spent over the journey from Fort William to Fort Augustus alone, as there are several fascinating digressions which you would miss if you tried to reach Kyle of Lochalsh in a day.

Our first halt is at the fifteenth-century Inverlochy Castle, barely a mile north of Fort William, near Lochy Bridge. Only a few crumbling walls are left, but it is a historic spot overlooking the scene where, in 1645, Montrose launched a surprise attack on the Covenanters. Argyll, chief of the Campbells, of whom the Covenanting army was largely composed, took himself off to a place of greater safety. Campbell of Auchinbreck was in command of his clansmen and put up a gallant fight, but his troops suffered defeat and he was slain. This was a great victory for Montrose, and his troops, comprising many Macdonalds, accounted for some 1500 of their foes at only slight cost to themselves.

Many tourists drive blithely up the Great Glen to Spean Bridge and Loch Lochy, and so miss one of the most fascinating and romantic excursions in this district. In order to follow this route we turn sharply to the left beyond Inverlochy Castle and cross Corpach Moss to Banavie. This is the start of the Glengarry route to the Isles, but once across the Caledonian Canal, instead of turning left to Corpach, we turn right to Banavie. A narrow but well-surfaced road follows the course of the Caledonian Canal to Gairlochy, giving extensive views towards the Ben Nevis massif with the River Lochy in the foreground.

Beyond Gairlochy the road continues along the west bank of Loch Lochy to Achnacarry and the finely timbered grounds of Achnacarry House. We should then return to Loch Lochy and follow a bad road which runs alongside the shores of the loch to Lunarkaig and Clunes, then turns inland and traverses the Mile Dorcha before continuing to Loch Arkaig and Achnasaul. There is a footpath from Achnasaul to Inverie by way of Glen Dessary, which gives a magnificent walk of nearly thirty miles through some of the wildest country in Scotland. As I have said, it is easier to reach Inverie on Loch Nevis by going by boat from Mallaig.

I drove to Achnasaul on a very wild and wet day, and found the four miles of rough pebbly track beyond Lunarkaig so bad that I should have done better to have walked. If time presses it is quicker to walk from Achnacarry House, but this will mean missing the Mile Dorcha, a magnificently wooded avenue, and the Falls of Cia-Aig. These are on the Mile Dorcha road, about quarter of a mile short of Loch Arkaig.

On my visit, the Cia-Aig falls were in spate—a splendid sight, enhanced by a rich setting of birch and hazel trees. Due to the wind and rain the waters of Loch Arkaig were quite choppy, and the view westwards towards a grim grey range of inhospitable mountains was wild and uninviting. I had thought of returning to Loch Lochy by the short cut to Achnacarry House, but was baulked by a narrow fragile bridge across the swollen waters of the River Arkaig. A notice proclaimed the bridge unsafe for cars, and I believed it.

This is Lochiel country, and Prince Charlie knew it well. There is a cave above the Mile Dorcha where he hid. At Murlaggan, near the head of Loch Arkaig, Jacobite treasure is said to be buried in the loch or in the ground nearby. If ever it should come to light it will probably comprise barrels of French gold. Seton Gordon gives a most informative account of this lovely district and its wild life in *Highways and Byways in the West Highlands*. It remains aloof and secluded due to its lack of roads, but no great hardship is involved in driving or walking as far as Achnasaul; and Loch Arkaig, the Cia-Aig Falls and the Mile Dorcha do at least give an introduction to this wonderful country.

Another beautiful scene is on the road from Gairlochy to Spean Bridge, viewed from the bridge above the Falls of Mucomir. The River Lochy, wide and stately, approaches from densely wooded surroundings and suddenly plunges headlong into the dark and sullen waters of the Spean. This rocky cataract is wild and tumultous and gives a savage glimpse of thundering, foam-flecked waters. The road spans the river immediately above the falls, and gives a magnificent view from the parapet of the bridge. This remarkable scene is within a couple of miles of the busy tourist route from Spean Bridge to Fort Augustus. The lower reaches of the Spean are far down in a thickly-wooded gorge, while the road high above gives stirring views of Ben Nevis and distant Lochaber. I can only urge you to take this road. Its beauties are of no common order.

The river is crossed at Spean Bridge by a solid, high-arched bridge giving a most engaging view of the dark-brown waters of the river and the lofty hills of Lochaber. Spean Bridge is at the junction of one of the very few roads crossing the mountain fastnesses of the Central Highlands. This fine main road links the Great North Road with the Great Glen, and in the thirty-five miles from Newtonmore to Spean Bridge gives varied scenes of loch and reservoir, mountain and moorland, glen and river.

This journey is beyond the scope of our tour of the western seaboard, but it is worth driving as far as Roy Bridge and Glen Spean. The parallel roads of Glen Roy can be seen from the rough track about four miles north of the main road at Roy Bridge. They consist of shelves or ledges formed by glacier ice, and show that at one time Glen Roy contained a great lake which sank in successive stages. The parallel roads thus show the outline of the lake at its various levels.

Beyond Roy Bridge the road enters Glen Spean, and the railway can be seen far down in the birch-festooned ravine near the rocky course of the River Spean. The gorge is particularly fine at Achluachrach, where you can descend to the footbridge spanning the river near the falls. The rocky bed of the river bears remarkable examples of water erosion with some particularly fine pot-holes.

The next stage of our tour follows the Great Glen from Loch Lochy to Loch Oich and Loch Ness. This is one of the most popular tourist routes in Scotland, and the splendid road surface is a boon to aged and careworn cars.

The road by Loch Lochy is more pleasant than impressive. The best view is across to Locheil Forest through a gap in the hills formed by Loch Arkaig. The Caledonian Canal is crossed at Laggan Drawbridge at the southern end of Loch Oich, and a short distance beyond that we come to the 'Well of the Heads', a conspicuous monument between road and loch.

When scanning the pages of Scottish history one is conscious of a long series of episodes of battle, murder and sudden death, and one feels that the chieftains of old must, in the main, have died at an early age. The name 'Well of the Heads' might have had no special significance in mere Sassenach country, but its Scottish significance is made plain for all to see. Lest there be any doubt about its awful history, the inscription on the well is printed in English, Gaelic, French and Latin, and as it speaks for itself, I will merely quote:

AS A MEMORIAL OF THE AMPLE AND SUMMARY VEN-GEANCE, WHICH IN THE SWIFT COURSE OF FEUDAL JUSTICE, INFLICTED BY THE ORDERS OF THE LORD McDONELL AND AROSS, OVERTOOK THE PERPETRATORS OF THE FOUL MURDER OF THE KEPPOCH FAMILY, A BRANCH OF THE POWERFUL AND ILLUSTRIOUS CLAN OF WHICH HIS LORD-SHIP WAS THE CHIEF, THIS MONUMENT IS ERECTED BY COLONEL McDONELL OF GLENGARRY XVII MAC-MHIC-ALAISTER HIS SUCCESSOR AND REPRESENTATIVE IN THE YEAR OF OUR LORD 1812. THE HEADS OF THE SEVEN MUR-DERERS WERE PRESENTED AT THE FEET OF THE NOBLE CHIEF IN GLENGARRY CASTLE AFTER HAVING BEEN WASHED IN THIS SPRING, AND EVER SINCE THAT EVENT WHICH TOOK PLACE IN THE SIXTEENTH CENTURY IT HAS BEEN KNOWN BY THE NAME OF 'TOBAR-NAN-CEANN' OR THE WELL OF THE HEADS.

We are now at the junction of the more northerly route to the Isles, and once committed to the far north-west the wide open spaces and sea-torn coastline of Wester Ross and Sutherland will be our lot. This vast and lonely region is penetrated by a few adventurous roads, some good and some bad, with several comfortable hotels well spaced between the various districts. No tourist should fail to visit this superbly beautiful region.

Before leaving the Great Glen it is worth continuing to Fort Augustus on the shores of Loch Ness. I admit that Loch Ness is a far cry from the western seaboard, but as we are compelled to travel at least as far north-east as Invergarry, it would be a pity to omit any chance, however slight, of seeing the world-famous monster. The thought of a telephoto of the Loch Ness monster has attracted me to this spot year after year, in fact ever since the elusive creature became world-famous.

While staying at Fort Augustus in the late summer of 1949 I was told at the hotel that the monster had been seen six weeks previously. In years gone by I had waited hopefully in the vicinity of Foyers or Castle Urquhart, a part of the loch said to be favoured by the monster. On this occasion I decided to climb a local hill and keep the whole loch under observation for an hour or two. Although it was a very clear day it seemed doubtful if I could do this, as Loch Ness is over twenty-two miles in length. The only likely hill was Creag Ard Achaidh, situated slightly to the south-east of Fort Augustus. Its summit was about a mile from the loch, but nearly 1400 feet above the water level. From this high viewpoint I would have a superb view.

I approached the hill from the finely constructed Foyers road, which starts near the Benedictine Monastery. It was an easy ascent, and from the summit I saw more of Loch Ness at once than ever before. I could just see the farthest reaches of the loch approaching Inverness, but a spur of an intervening hill cut off the Dores district. The water lay still as glass, and I could distinguish reflections of the trees at the head of the loch near Fort Augustus. Streaks and smears on the surface of the loch many miles distant were clearly visible, indicating that steamers or boats had gone by fairly recently. It was warm, clear and sunny, with hardly a breath of wind even at my airy viewpoint. Conditions were perfect for the monster, but I need hardly add that my vigil was unrewarded. I recommend this viewpoint to other enthusiasts. With powerful glasses to magnify the more distant portions of the loch, this would seem as good an observation post as any. At the worst, there is a magnificent view of the Great Glen not only towards Loch Ness but also to the south-west towards Lochiel.

The monster has been seen and described by so many reliable witnesses that it is untenable to say blandly 'they are all mistaken'. The balance of opinion seems to indicate a creature about forty-five to fifty feet in length with a long neck, a tapering and pointed tail, and a head not much wider than its body. The lengthy body can be contorted into humps and is dark brown in colour. It has been suggested that the monster is a survival of the plesiosaurus, a prehistoric creature supposedly extinct. It is said to have a remarkable turn of speed, and its long and flexible neck would certainly be handy for darting at prey. The plesiosauria were great fish-eaters, and had numerous sharp teeth, ideal for holding slippery squirming prey. So far as I can ascertain the plesiosaurus rarely exceeded a length of twenty feet, but its near relation—the elasmosaurus—attained a length of forty-five feet. It is interesting to note that marine reptiles of this kind may at times visit the land. It seems self-evident that all those adventurous people who set forth blithely to meet the monster may have to do some quick thinking if their wish is granted.

I have made at least a dozen visits to Loch Ness without seeing the monster, but on nearly every occasion I collected accounts of its presence. Perhaps the most interesting story was from a lady at Fort Augustus who, in 1934, told me that her husband had encountered the creature when rowing on the loch. From all I could gather, once he had seen its two or three black humps coming to the surface near his boat, his only desire was to get back to land with the utmost speed. The monster is certainly accepted by the local inhabitants. No doubt the mystery will be solved in time, but there is little point in ridiculing the evidence of hundreds of eye-witnesses.

You can drive to the Kyle of Lochalsh from Invermoriston, this being the more convenient approach from Inverness, but our route from Fort Augustus gives more widespread views. Both roads converge at Cluanie Bridge.

We leave the Invergarry Hotel and follow the long road westwards. The entire route from Invergarry to Kyle of Lochalsh is now along a good, tarred road. For the first ten miles you will enjoy views of the imposing peaks of the Glengarry Forest, the fine birch trees found in such profusion in the glen, the placid reaches of Loch Garry and the cascading course of the river. Beyond Tomdoun an adventurous road continues westwards to Loch Quoich and Kinlochhourn. The return journey involves thirty-two miles of bad road, and a full day would be needed to do the trip justice. The nearest accommodation is at the Tomdoun Hotel.

The present road from Tomdoun to Glen Loyne and over the moors to Cluanie Bridge is a great improvement on the original stony track, and would now be an easy route for a stream of motor coaches, although the surroundings are still as desolate as ever. After crossing the River Loyne near Loch Loyne the road enters Ross-shire, gradually climbing in the direction of the peaks of the Cluanie Forest.

Be sure to halt at the top of the pass and look back to Glen Loyne and range after range of distant mountains. This is an exceptionally lonely view, with no sign of human habitation, and if you should be here in wild weather the scene is one of the most desolate in the Highlands. Even on a fine clear day there is nothing but sombre silence, great brooding mountains and barren moor. The view from the descent to Cluanie Bridge is more majestic and stimulating. You can see a dozen or more peaks over 3000 feet in height, and many are over 3600 feet. Garbh Leac is almost directly opposite, Loch Cluanie and the Invermoriston road are seen extending for miles to the east, and the wild peaks around Glen Shiel are visible to the west.

The roads descend by easy gradients to Cluanie Bridge, where you will find Cluanie Inn, a well-known haven for explorers of this remote district. Beyond the inn, the road to the west soon descends to Glen Shiel amid mountain scenery of the highest order. The Five Sisters of Kintail guard the glen to the east, and the mountains to the immediate west, culminating in the Saddle, add further majesty to the scene. Sgurr Ouran, the highest of the Five Sisters, reaches a height of 3505 feet, and competes with the Saddle to dwarf the diminutive road which creeps furtively through the glen here almost at sea level. The deep corries, vast deer forests and serrated peaks make this an awe-inspiring journey even today. In 1773 the redoubtable Dr Johnson was impressed, and it was here that he first conceived his *Journey to the Western Islands*.

The Kintail Lodge Hotel at Invershiel is a good base for Mam Rattachan, a notorious hill between Loch Duich and the Sound of Sleat at Glenelg. This used to be the Road to the Isles in Dr Johnson's time, and was frequently used by motorists before the war, when there was a car ferry across to Kylerhea in Skye. The ferry was subsequently suspended, but comparatively recently re-opened for use in the summer months on weekdays only. I have not been along this route since 1949 when the road surface was in very poor condition, being loose and gravelly, but whatever its condition I should hesitate to call this a motoring road in the usual touring sense of the word, as the ascent of Mam Rattachan involves a very winding climb from sea level to a height of 1116 feet with a maximum gradient of 1 in 5. The road rises over 1000 feet in just under two miles. I made the ascent on a very hot day, and my car found it a very punishing climb.

The view across Loch Duich to the Five Sisters of Kintail is one of the most famous and magnificent panoramas in Scotland. It is rather a surprise view, because the ascent is made deep through the heart of an afforestation scheme. The descent to Glenelg is more gradual, with rugged views across the Sound of Sleat to the mountains of Skye. There are two well-preserved Iron Age brochs within easy reach of Glenelg. You will have to return the same way, unless you cross to Skye, and the descent to Loch Duich is mildly sensational, as the loch appears to be 1100 feet below the offside mudguard. But the tree-line is soon reached, and exerts a soothing influence.

The road from Invershiel to Dornie Bridge passes through magnificent scenery. At first the road winds round Loch Duich to Croe Bridge, and then follows the northern shore of the loch to Kintail Church, Inverinate and Keppoch. The views from the highest point on the road at Keppoch are outstanding, and the scene looking back to Loch Duich and the Five Sisters of Kintail is nearly as fine as the view from Mam Rattachan.

Further on you can see Loch Alsh, Skye, Eilean Donan Castle and the remote fastnesses of Loch Long. Eilean Donan, with its castle linked to the mainland by a bridge, enjoys an enviable position. Restoration of the castle was completed in 1932 after 20 years work, and its imposing beauty and dignity are a delight to see. There are fascinating glimpses of the castle from the roadside all along this route. To those who suffered the dangers of

oh Ailort Inn

INVERNESS-SHIRE

nfinnan—
nce Charlie's
nument

Sgurr Ouran an
the Saddle from
near Shiel Bridg

GLENSHIEL—ROSS-SHIRE

Loch Duich ar
Five Sisters of
tail from the
of Mam Ratta

the old Dornie Ferry at low water, the new bridge must be a godsend.

A rough road, part of it privately owned, extends along the northern shore of Loch Long to Killilan and Glen Elchaig, from where the Falls of Glomach can be reached. Another route to the falls is from Croe Bridge. The wild and lonely hill path from Croe Bridge over the Bealach na Sroine (the 'Coffin Road') involves a return tramp of over ten miles, and a climb of 2000 feet. The Falls of Glomach are less than two miles from the Glen Elchaig track, and this would seem the obvious choice. Unfortunately, numerous intervening streams and rivers have to be crossed, and the path to the falls is not all easy going, except to the experienced walker. However, the Falls of Glomach are well worth a visit, as their unbroken plunge for 370 feet is said to be the highest in Britain.

We follow the main road to the west, with its enticing glimpses of the jagged peaks of the Cuillin of Skye across the broad expanse of Loch Alsh. The road from Balmacara to Kyle of Lochalsh, although a main road, picks its way with such delicacy, and is so tortuous, that there is little opportunity to enjoy the views across to Skye without halting. The road approaches the railway on reaching the western shores of the peninsula at Erbusaig, and, as usual, the railway has pride of place. Nevertheless you will enjoy fine views across to Scalpay, Blaven and the Red Hills and Cuillin of Skye. And so we come to the busy little village and railway terminus of Kyle, the gateway to Skye.

CHAPTER TWELVE

THE ISLE OF SKYE

K YLE OF LOCHALSH is a concentrated little place. There is not much of it, and the population is only about 500, but you will find a palatial railway hotel, the railway terminus, many shops, another hotel and various garages. There is a car-ferry across to Kyleakin in Skye, an island where you do not have to be a rock-climber to find excitement.

Kyleakin is a likeable village with whitewashed houses, a quaint harbour, good hotels and the nearby ruins of Castle Maoil, said to have been built by 'Saucy Mary', a Norse King's daughter who married a Mackinnon. She is reputed to have stretched a chain across the narrows of the Kyle near the castle, thus preventing the passage of ships until they had paid toll.

The best road in Skye encourages swift progress to Broadford, and one approaches the Red Hills with increasing excitement. I was almost sorry when I reached the road junction near Broadford and turned southwards along a bleak and barren route, which did not improve until I came to the woods and gardens of the Duisdale Hotel. The view from the lawn of this hotel looks straight into the mouth of Loch Hourn, and anything more striking I have rarely seen. Ben Sgriol dominates the scene to the north of the loch, and Ladhar Bheinn guards its southern shores. It was a mild sunny evening with slight haze, and the scene had that strange ethereal quality which distinguishes the landscapes of the old masters. The delicate tracery of the distant rugged slopes had all the witchery of illusion. The colouring was wonderful. There was nothing spectacular or dramatic about it, but rather a consummate beauty and perfect harmony which held one spellbound.

Later that evening I climbed a hill overlooking the Sound of Sleat. This, too, was a wonderful scene. I could see Isle Oronsay with its adjacent light-house and the whitewashed houses of the tiny village. The mouth of Loch Hourn was now nearer, and there seemed an awful loneliness about it as it lay cradled between its attendant mountains. Approaching dusk was slowly

Cape Wrath

NLOCH ERVIE

Laxford Bridge

urie

NORTH MINCH

Scourie

Laxford Bridge

SUTHERLAND

LOCHINVER

Loch Shin

To Lairg

Achiltibuie

ULLAPOOL

Loch Broom

R. Broom

To Garve

Uig

Loch Ewe

Poolewe

Gair Loch

GAIRLOCH

Loch Maree

ROSS & CROMARTY

To Dingwall

Loch Torridon

Kinlochewe

L. Rosque

Achnasheen

nvegan

PORTREE

Sound of Raasay

Raasay

Applecross

Glen Carron

SKYE

Glen Affric

The Cuillin

L. Coruisk

Kyle of Lochalsh

Strome Ferry

Kyleakin

Broadford

Glenelg

R. Morison

FORT AUGUSTUS

Cuillin Sound

L. Scovaig

L. Slapin

Sound of Sleat

Invergarry

L. Oich

Rum

MALLAIG

Glen Garry

INVERNESS

R. Gorry

Loch Arkaig

draining the beauty away, and a breath of cold night air warned me that it was time to go.

I awakened next day to a morning of tropical heat. Visibility was limited by haze, and I found it hard to believe this was the Isle of Skye, notorious for its rain and mist. I made an early departure and headed northwards. The Sound of Sleat had almost Mediterranean colouring.

I came to the long straggling village of Broadford, lying in magnificent surroundings. The Red Hills to the west, Beinn na Caillich to the east and the Applecross mountains of the mainland to the north—all these lend excitement to the scene and urge one ever onward. It is the same all the way to Sligachan, with lonely views of bog and moorland dominated by the Red Hills, and later, the great peaks of Blaven, Marsco and Glamaig. Occasional crofts and houses, notably at Strollamus, and shaggy Highland cattle, impart warmth to the route, making a wonderful introduction to the subsequent marvels of Skye. The scene is especially savage and lonely at the head of Loch Ainort, where the road seems a puny thing dwarfed by the grandeur of the mountains. Then, like an oasis in the wilderness, comes Sligachan Hotel, one of the best known hotels in Britain—I am tempted to say, in the world.

From Sligachan I decided to drive to Portree by the west coast road, which would take me to Dunvegan Castle. Although I had seven or eight hours in which to cover the fifty miles of bad road, with frequent halts for photography I should have little enough time. It was so hot that I wore shirt and trousers and little else, driving with the roof, windscreen and all windows wide open. This was the hottest day I have ever known in Skye, and clouds of white dust trailed behind the car. I halted near Drynoch, where the road winds round two corries, and climbed a hill giving a superb view of the Cuillin. The heat haze and absence of clouds detracted considerably from the majesty of the scene, but in clear weather this is one of the best views of the Cuillin. It was rather exciting to know that I was now farther west than any part of the British mainland.

Plate 54. Eilean Donan Castle and Loch Duich, Wester Ross

MALLAIG—ISLE OF SKYE, INVERNESS-SHIRE

On the western side of Loch Harport, at Carbost quite near to Drynoch, is a place of great interest to connoisseurs of whisky—the famous Talisker Distillery. Talisker itself is a tiny coastal hamlet, near some of the most tremendous cliffs in Britain. A slight glimpse of their lofty precipices is visible from Loch Beag near Bracadale, but like the superb cliffs of western Duirinish they are more conveniently seen from the sea. Some of the cliffs attain a tremendous height, but are not easily accessible from land or sea.

The bumpy road led ever westwards, and with the intense heat and boiling engine I missed the ruins of Dun Beag, one of the best brochs to be found in Skye. I stopped at St. John's Chapel at the lonely head of Loch Caroy. The church was in a ruinous condition, but the graveyard was well tended. Several graves were covered with flowers. Surrounding trees, not yet in leaf, promised restful shade in summer. A crofter's cottage stood nearby, and its thatched roof was firmly lashed to withstand the fury of the gales and storms which often sweep across this remote region. I could now see Macleod's Tables, the flat-topped hills of Duirinish, and at length reached the westernmost point of our tour at Dunvegan.

Dunvegan Castle was closed to visitors on this occasion, but I spent a leisurely hour walking round the grounds and down to the beach near the little pier. It was delightful in the woods and gardens, but I remember best the scene as I stood on the small tree-covered promontory and looked across the narrow creek to the grey walls and frowning battlements of this ancient building.

Dunvegan Castle has been the seat of the Macleods since the thirteenth century, but part of the keep is said to date from the ninth century. The castle is magnificently preserved, and has an air of ancient splendour which well repays a visit. You can see the interior on Tuesday and Thursday afternoons. I had been round the castle before, and remembered many of its treasures, including the Fairy Flag, the Dunvegan Cup, Rory Mor's Horn, letters from Dr Johnson and Sir Walter Scott giving thanks for past hospitality, and the wonderful paintings by Raeburn and Ramsay of former Macleods and their wives. There are hosts of other precious relics, as well as a Fairy Tower and a most gloomy dungeon.

The *Brattach Sith*, or Fairy Flag, is the most famous relic, and its tattered brown silk and crimson 'elf spots' may have an eastern origin, as it is feasible that the flag was originally brought from the crusades. According to tradition the flag was given to the fourth chief by his fairy wife, who told him that it had power to save the Macleod clan upon three occasions if waved at a time of need. The flag has so far been waved twice, and on both occasions it brought victory to the Macleods in battle. It is thought that its presence saved the castle from destruction by fire in 1938. Rory Mor's drinking-horn was used as a test of manhood, and each heir had to empty it at a single draught. As it held half a gallon of claret this feat must have required considerable practice.

It was now evening, and time to be moving. I found the road rather dreary and barren until reaching Bernisdale and the adjacent woods near Droehaid. It was pleasant to find trees in Skye, and the road forward to Carbost near the head of Loch Snizort Beag had a quiet and restful attraction. It was near Carbost that I came across one of the trimmest and neatest crofters' cottages I have seen. With its thatched roof and whitewashed walls it made an enchanting picture. Even the chimney was thatched, and the roof, as on other primitive cottages of this type, was supported by ropes from which heavy stones were suspended. The crofters' cottages and 'black-houses' of the Hebrides are essentially primitive, but they are constructed with great solidity, and designed to withstand the wildest weather.

Portree is the only town in Skye. Although many old houses surround the harbour, most of the town is on higher ground. There are shops, hotels, garages and even trees. You can see the site of a room at the Royal Hotel where Prince Charlie is reputed to have said farewell to Flora Macdonald; otherwise there is little of interest. But Portree is an excellent centre for touring, and many bus and taxi excursions are available to every corner of the island.

During the night a westerly gale descended upon Skye, and I awoke to a cold wretched morning of drenching rain. The contrast to the previous day of tropical heat seemed incredible, and as I splashed along to Sligachan muffled in a thick overcoat there seemed little hope of any improvement in the weather. Sgurr nan Gillean was wrapped in thick mist, and the prospect was bleak, desolate, and exceedingly wet.

During my stay at Sligachan the wind increased in velocity, and I became used to awakening to the noise of hail beating on the roof of my attic bedroom. I felt disinclined to go out, but at length conscience prompted me to visit Loch Coruisk, and I booked a passage on a coach trip from Portree to Elgol. The coach had to pass Sligachan Hotel, where I would meet it. It was a boisterous morning with heavy squalls, strong wind and bouncing hail.

I sat in the hotel porch waiting for the coach. Eventually, long after I was due to leave, a taxi pulled up and the driver said that due to the bad weather there was no enthusiasm for the Loch Coruisk trip, and as there were only two other passengers we had been conceded a large and comfortable taxi. The delay was due to the taxi having hit a rock on the Portree to Staffin route, which had damaged the sump.

The driver warned me not to take my own car on this notorious road from Portree to Staffin. I think every motor mechanic on the island must have given me this warning. I was told that sheep could be lost in the potholes, and that even the local buses were dying a hideous death. One garage proprietor said he would refuse to repair my car if I attempted the road!

As we sped along the edge of the unguarded cliffs of Loch Ainort I felt disinclined for conversation, but the driver knew the road blindfolded, and explained that he was trying to regain lost time, otherwise the boatman would have left when we reached Elgol.

There was a good road all the way to Torrin, and the scenery would have been magnificent in fine weather. The road from Torrin to Elgol had all the qualities of a river-bed fast approaching a condition of spate, and now I saw the advantages of exceptionally large balloon tyres. The driver knew just how to fling the car on to the most suitable pebbles with the least damage, and we bumped and splashed along to Elgol in commendable time.

We halted at the brink of a precipitous path to the beach and inquired if the boatman had left. We were told that he was at a funeral, and that we had little hope of crossing Loch Scavaig. Our obliging driver said that he would wait an hour or two, and, as the weather had improved to the extent of not actually raining, I set off along the path to Camasunary and climbed a nearby hill. As I had surmised, it was possible to see Loch Coruisk beyond

Loch Scavaig. A pall of dark clouds hung over the Cuillin, and the scene was one of savage magnificence. I could see much of Blaven, Clach Glas, distant Marsco, and the white cottage at Camasunary. To the south-west Rum was almost completely hidden in dark swirling storm-clouds. I hoped they would stay there.

I returned to Elgol, and came to a delightful cottage in an exquisite situation. It had whitewashed walls, a slated roof and a lawn built out to form a terrace overlooking Loch Scavaig, nearly 400 feet beneath. Over the door were the words *Grand View*. Miss Mackinnon greeted me as an old friend, and showed me into the parlour, where I should not have been surprised to have seen a portrait of Queen Victoria occupying the place of honour. Instead, an enormous autographed portrait of Patricia Roc dominated the room and aroused all my latent curiosity. As I toyed with a light snack of bacon, fried eggs and potatoes, jam, wheaten scones, rock-buns and tea, Miss Mackinnon ventured to explain. It seemed that in the film *The Brothers* (from the novel by L. A. G. Strong) scenes were taken in this locality, and the members of the cast were frequent visitors at her cottage. In fact they had all written their autographs on the wall near the door. Solemnly I photographed this piece of documentary history.

Miss Mackinnon was just saying that Patricia Roc, 'such a charming lassie', had sat at my table for seven weeks, when, on looking through the window, I noticed a black speck on the water heading for Loch Coruisk. Our driver then rushed in to say that the boatman had returned and I had missed the boat.

This was too much! Hastily cramming the last rock-bun into its appointed channels, I grabbed my cameras and rushed off, leaving Miss Mackinnon wondering whether the talkative gentleman would come back to pay for his lunch. I do not know what the record is for descending the cliff path at Elgol, but I should think I hold it. I remember shouting 'Boat Ahoy' at the top of my voice, thereby inducing the fear of death into a herd of panic-stricken cattle. I came to halt at the edge of seaweed-strewn rocks, over which the tide was swilling in a cold and sullen manner.

The boatman returned, and as I jumped from the rocks I remembered that Patricia Roc had found it very chilly swimming in this part of the ocean during the filming of *The Brothers*. I spent the next quarter of an hour regaining my breath, while we slipped along the choppy waters of Loch Scavaig. The dirty weather which had been giving Rum such a trouncing was now sweeping in our wake, and I hoped that we should reach Loch Coruisk before the deluge. It seemed doubtful; our tiny motor launch took time over the five-mile crossing, and I had opportunity to look for the 'Bad Step' on the grim slopes of Sgurr-an-Strudhidh.

We tied up near the River Scavaig, and I darted ahead to cross the neck of land separating Loch Coruisk from the sea. If there was a path I missed it, and soon found myself crawling across the slippery rocks known to climbers as boiler-plates. I found the steep gabbro slopes a shade less unpleasant, but by the time I stood above Loch Coruisk my shoes were in a state from which they never recovered.

It was a wretched day, and Loch Coruisk had none of the dramatic grandeur which it possesses in fine weather. The mist hung low and the steep walls of this rocky amphitheatre gave the appearance of some hellish cauldron unsuited to mere mortals.

Loch Scavaig was developing some fair-sized breakers as we returned through drenching rain to Elgol, and, if I had not already been well saturated by the rain, the spray from the waves would have done the job just as well. Once you are thoroughly soaked to the skin, it is not a bad feeling, and my only concern was for my cameras.

I felt quite happy on the long climb to *Grand View* cottage, and the interested cattle were obviously contrasting my headlong descent with my slow and laborious ascent. Miss Mackinnon had tea waiting, and I discovered a new and ferocious appetite.

By the time I had eaten the last cake and drunk the final cup of tea, settled my account with Miss Mackinnon, and promised to come again, it seemed doubtful if we should be back in Sligachan before dark. But our driver was a wizard at the wheel, and despite my insistence in stopping to photograph Blaven from Torrin we covered the thirty-three miles in remarkable time.

Next morning, feeling decidedly stiff and hungry, I listened to the hail on my window and decided to visit Rudha Hunish, the most northerly tip of Skye. I told the receptionist that if I did not return my address would be the 'Quiraing'. The garage proprietor at Portree thought otherwise. He peered underneath the car, said 'Whist!', and drew my attention to the track-rod between the front wheels, which was bent to a perfect curve.

I had lunch at the Royal Hotel, and returned to the garage at 3 p.m. to find the car repaired. There was now a formidable gale which fairly shook the car as I bumped northwards alongside the shores of Loch Snizort. Lingering clouds had no chance against such a gale, and eventually the sun came out and visibility was excellent. Uig Bay looked magnificent. I had trouble with a bad hairpin bend at Idrigil, but soon afterwards encountered one of the best roads in Skye, just where I should have expected the worst. This continued to Staffin Bay, but it is not a route I can recommend in a hurricane. Under better weather conditions this would be a superb drive.

Flora Macdonald's grave, situated in the burial-ground of Kilmuir, was my first pilgrimage. A tall Celtic Cross marks her resting-place. The view from the graveside is inexpressibly lonely and magnificent. I could see the coastline towards Rudha Hunish, the island of Fladda Chuain, and the long line of distant hills from Uist to Harris and Lewis.

Then I continued towards Duntulm. The road descended to the shore, where heavy seas lashed in fury against fallen heaps of rock broken off from the steep cliffs, which towered in awful splendour high above the roadside. Rudha Hunish looked black and sinister, but the ruins of Duntulm Castle shone brightly in fitful sunlight. I halted above Duntulm Lodge, now a hotel, and wished there were time to stay there. A few fishing boats lay uneasily at anchor near a rocky islet, and I could see Fladda far out to sea.

As I approached Staffin I passed several lonely crofts, 'black-houses', and stacks of peat making an appropriate foreground to the fantastic peaks of the Quiraing, and the grim heights of the distant Storr. A belt of dark storm clouds swept across Trotternish, but the sun still shone around my northern viewpoint. Rarely have I seen a more breath-taking or awe-inspiring scene.

I halted by some peat-stacks and shielings at Staffin, and deliberated what best to do. I had been warned that even if my car survived the appalling road to Portree, the journey would take several hours due to having to drive at walking pace. On the other hand the gale was now approaching hurricane force, and I was not enthusiastic about the exposed cliffs of Score Bay—and even Uig Bay might give trouble. I decided to risk the coast road along the cliffs, and duly returned to Score Bay.

Huge foam-flecked breakers were thundering on the shore, and the lofty pillared cliffs gave the scene a truly majestic appearance. The road maintains a fairly low level for the first mile or so, and then gradually climbs to about 250 feet, with little or no protection from the awful plunge into the sea. It was most unpleasant. The wind tore at the car, and a lighter model might well have overturned. I was glad when the road turned inland and southwards.

I stopped at Idrigil and found a comparatively sheltered viewpoint overlooking the crofts and whitewashed cottages dotted around Uig Bay. The view westwards across Loch Snizort to the Ascrib Islands and the long outline of Vaternish showed gale-swept waters at times flooded with silver light. The cliff road south of Uig Bay was not quite as trying as the Score Bay route, and the car did not rock quite so heavily in the tearing wind. I ran into a hail-storm approaching Loch Snizort Beag, and had a decidedly cheerless journey along the bumpy road to Portree.

Beyond Portree I looked back towards the fine weather and the tremendous cliffs fronting the Sound of Raasay. When the coast road is repaired between Portree and Staffin the motorist will be able to obtain closer glimpses of the strange pinnacle called the Old Man of Storr, the stupendous cliffs along the coast, and the Kilt Rock. The hill-track from Staffin to Uig is another route giving fine views of the Quiraing.

Bad weather continued, and I spent the rest of my time in Skye dodging hail showers and torrential rain, while the Cuillin hid their savage peaks in swirling clouds. I did manage a return trip from Broadford to Torrin and had a wonderful view of a rain-storm sweeping across from Blaven. As I looked back from the reed-strewn shores of Loch Kilchrist, I could see the drenching rain obliterating hill after hill. I stopped again to inspect the ruins and scattered graveyard of the ancient church of Kilchrist, of which only the gables and ivy-covered walls remain. St. Maelrubha came from Applecross to preach here in the seventh century.

The landscape soon became effaced by torrential rain, and I had no chance to visit the ruins of Coire-chat-achan, where Dr Johnson and Boswell were so hospitably and divertingly entertained in 1773.

During my short stay in Skye I had seen the island in all its moods. Tropical heat, mist and rain, storm and tempest had all come my way, and I had known glorious intervals of sunshine and dazzling colour. In spite of a good deal of effort I had been unable to visit all the roads in Skye, and you need only read *The Misty Isle of Skye* by J. A. MacCulloch, to realise how much I missed during my visit. In justification of this brief account I can only urge you not to omit any of the routes I have described. They serve as a fitting introduction to an island of rare magic.

CHAPTER THIRTEEN

LOCH ALSH TO LOCH TORRIDON

MUCH of the Kyle peninsula now belongs to the National Trust, and is comprised in an 8000-acre estate, extending from Loch Carron to Loch Alsh, and including the village of Plockton, part of Kyle, and Balmacara House. The district is one of great natural beauty. You will be delighted with Plockton, a beautifully situated crofting village surrounded by rugged hills, often thickly wooded and facing the splendour of the Applecross mountains. Some day there may be a motoring road from Plockton to Strome Ferry along the southern shore of Loch Carron. At present there is a track of sorts, which various maps relegate to the ambiguous category of 'other roads'. Sometimes roads marked in this way turn out to be practicable for cars, but this is a route only suitable for the walker.

The road from Loch Alsh to Strome Ferry is quite good. The state of the tide involved an awkward angle between ferry and jetty, and the car exhaust and undercarriage received further unkind scrapes on disembarking. Should you possess a long car with a low ground clearance and considerable overhang, it might be desirable to wait for high tide before attempting some of the more troublesome West Highland ferries. They are always worst at low tide. Strome Ferry can be avoided by entraining your car at Kyle and travelling by rail to Strathcarron. If only there were a road from Strome Ferry to Strathcarron, following the line of the railway, Lochalsh and the Island of Skye would be much more accessible to tourists. In common with the Kyle of Lochalsh and Kylerhea ferries, Strome Ferry does not operate on Sundays. Skye is completely isolated from the mainland from the last ferry on Saturday evenings to the first ferry on Monday mornings.

I halted beside the fragment of Strome Castle, and looked towards the Cuillin nearly thirty miles beyond the silvery waters of Loch Carron. Heavy rain was approaching from the north-west. The Cuillin were gradually obliterated, and the glittering water of the loch turned to a dull and dismal grey. I continued to the picturesque and curiously named village of Jeantown (or Lochcarron), consisting of a long line of houses on the waterfront.

There are two justly famous excursions from Lochcarron, and it is worth staying a day or two at the hotel in order to allow adequate time for a leisurely survey of the magnificent scenery on both routes. The easier excursion is to Kishorn, Shieldaig and Loch Torridon. There is a good road as far as Shieldaig, beyond where the track is best followed on foot. The return journey is about thirty miles. The other excursion also takes us to Kishorn, and then diverges from Tornapress to Applecross, traversing the Bealach-na-Ba or 'Pass of the Cattle'. Applecross is about eighteen miles from Strathcarron, and the last twelve miles are the toughest on any motoring road in Britain, as we shall see.

A steep road turns west from Lochcarron, climbing over the hills to Kishorn, a most delightful haven on the shores of Loch Kishorn. There is a wonderful view across to the Applecross mountains, and as you sit on the green machair between loch and road, I think you will agree that this is one of the most hauntingly beautiful scenes we have yet encountered. If you keep quite still, hosts of rabbits will come out to keep you company.

A little to the north of this viewpoint is a forlorn signpost bearing the magic word 'Applecross', and pointing along a narrow lane to the west. Tornapress, which appears to be a solitary house, is a few yards to the north. Ignore for the present the subtle temptation of the Applecross road, and continue northwards through Glen Shieldaig to the small fishing village of Shieldaig. The Vikings gave the name 'herring bay' to this remote village sheltered between rocky hills. The houses are built close to the pebbly beach, and I noticed the skeleton of a derelict ship, whose grim gaunt outline added a touch of desolation to the scene. A few boats were drawn up on the beach, and several fishing nets were hung up to dry. There is a small inn, a post office and one or two shops.

This tiny village has an almost Hebridean atmosphere, and if you like to get away from the world the attractions of Shieldaig are almost Utopian. You may be able to hire a boat to visit Loch Torridon, but a short walk of half a mile will bring you within sight of Upper Loch Torridon. This is approached by a very rough road, passable for cars, leading to the east and over the neck of the intervening peninsula, separating Upper Loch Torridon from Loch Shieldaig.

The mountains were heavy with cloud, and rain was approaching as I tramped along this lonely road. Both Ben Alligin and Liathach were shrouded in mist, and presented a desolate and sombre sight. But on a clear sunny day the reddish peaks of Torridonian sandstone, tipped here and there with gleaming quartzite, make an impressive scene. These great mountains of primeval rock date from the beginning of the world.

Loch Torridon is best approached from Kinlochewe, and it is a great pity that there is no through road for the motorist between Shieldaig and the head of Upper Loch Torridon. The distance is only seven miles, and comprises one of the finest walks in the Highlands.

We can now consider the road from Tornapress to Applecross over the Bealach-na-Ba. This involves surmounting the longest hill in Britain, the gradient being the least of the difficulties. Perhaps it would be best to tell you about the hill, describe my own ascent, and then it will be up to you to decide to go or not.

The climb starts at sea level at Tornapress, and winds to the top of the Bealach-na-Ba, reaching a height of 2054 feet. Most of the ascent is covered in five miles, with a descent of similar length to Applecross, also at sea level. If you drive to Applecross the return must be made the same way, which means that you will have to climb and descend 4108 feet in twenty-four miles. Although the gradient rarely exceeds 1 in 5, there is no other climb of comparable severity in Britain. The difficulties are due to the length of the hill, a stony surface barely car width, lack of passing places, and a high grass-covered ridge in the middle of the road, which would catch the undercarriage of cars having a low clearance.

The climb increases in severity, and culminates in several acute hairpin bends of such difficulty that only small cars can negotiate them without reversing. There are poorly guarded drops from the roadside, sometimes to a depth of several hundred feet. In short, this pass is much more severe than the usual 'difficult' touring and motoring roads, and once committed to the route the road is too narrow to turn back. If you have a small but powerful car with high ground clearance, if you enjoy adventurous roads and have a head for heights, you will find the journey to be magnificent motoring. But be sure to choose fine weather. Mist, snow or ice would be highly dangerous obstacles.

Don't think I am discouraging you from visiting the bealach and its fine views—possibly the finest in Britain. If you feel disinclined to take your car, the twelve-mile return walk is well worth the effort.

Most of us have had minor ambitions of one sort or another. One of mine was to visit the bealach at sunset, and I cherished this ambition for twenty years, waiting for the right conditions. It was, therefore, a solemn moment when I arrived at Tornapress about an hour and a half before sunset, and turned along the Applecross road. It was cold, but there was good visibility. I crossed the River Kishorn and drove along a narrow track, climbing steadily above the shores of the loch.

The road at first seemed as if it might climb the deep valley between the towering slopes of Beinn Bhan and Sgurr a' Chaorachain, but soon headed seawards and emerged high above Loch Kishorn. This was a trying part of my journey; the surface was stony and the high ridge in the middle of the road proved troublesome to my car.

The view was already breath-taking, and extended beyond Loch Kishorn to Loch Carron and the Plockton district. As I climbed higher, the road entered a magnificent corrie guarded on one side by the tremendous cliffs of Meall Gorm, and on the other by the steep screes of Sgurr a' Chaorachain. For the next two miles the road crept up the side of this mountain, and became an exciting scree traverse. I am glad to say that the troublesome centre ridge gradually disappeared from the road and the surface improved.

There are wonderful views of the precipitous bastion of Meall Gorm immediately opposite and only a few hundred feet distant. This great cliff is first seen when the road is a mere 800 feet above sea level, and, as the cliff top must be nearly 2000 feet in height, its dramatic appearance, especially when flooded with golden sunlight, is unforgettable. Yet the summit of the Bealach-na-Ba actually overlooks the top of these great cliffs.

Once the upper amphitheatre is reached, the climb is less steep for a short distance, and there are not such breath-taking drops from the roadside. But this respite is short-lived, and a steep ascent leads to the first and most formidable of the hairpin bends, the difficulties of which increase in proportion to the length of the car. If you have a long car this stage of the climb will be the worst. I succeeded at the third attempt, finding it very difficult as I had no passenger to direct reversing operations. The next two hairpin bends were difficult but not nearly so troublesome.

I reached the bealach after an hour of continuous low-gear driving from Tornapress. Fortunately the temperature was near freezing point, and the radiator never had a chance to boil. I began the descent to Applecross, hoping to see a sunset over the Cuillin twenty-four miles away, but was surprised to note a severe snow-storm swirling round their serrated outline. At such a distance the Cuillin appeared quite dwarfed, and seemed much less in height than the summit of the Bealach-na-Ba. I viewed this snow-storm with some concern. If it swept eastwards the bealach would become impassable, and I should be marooned at Applecross until conditions improved. I decided to return to Lochcarron that night, and it was as well I did. Next morning the bealach was hidden in mist and was snowbound.

Before returning to Loch Kishorn I stopped at the top of the steep descent to the hairpin bends. This is the finest viewpoint of all, and no words can describe the wonder of it as the setting sun filled the great corrie with golden splendour. The cliffs of Meall Gorm seemed to blaze with light, and every detail of the rocks could be seen with amazing clarity. This is an incomparable view. When seen under such ideal conditions its sublime grandeur will haunt you for the rest of your life. I have seen the awful desolation of the ice-bound peaks of northern Iceland, the splendour of the Atlas Mountains in North Africa, the wonder of the snowbound Sierra Nevada in southern Spain and the magic of sunsets from the summit of the Rock of Gibraltar. But none of these scenes, wonderful though they be, can compare with the majesty of this view from the Bealach-na-Ba. We have seen many fine views on this tour, but even Mam Rattachan, Skye and Glencoe must take second place to the bealach.

I stayed until the sunset had faded away. The silence was awesome, and as I stood in complete solitude I might have been the last man on earth. The only sound on my long descent was the crackle of pebbles under the tyres, and it was an eerie experience gazing at the screes above and below. The countless thousands of boulders poised high above seemed on the verge of crashing down. I slid stealthily down the hill at the merest crawl, and it was dark when I reached Lochcarron.

Next morning the mountains were snow-capped and it was bitterly cold, with a wind of gale force, and squalls. The sun shone between the torrential showers, and visibility was wonderful. It is a pleasure to be on the road under such conditions.

Jeantown sparkled in the morning sunlight, and the surrounding hills were dappled with shadows from wind-tossed clouds. Here and there some distant snow-capped peak would attract an extra dark cloud, and soon become effaced in swirling rain. Such heavy showers, intense though they were, never lasted long, and did little to spoil my journey up Glen Carron to Achnasheen. This glen is very alpine in character, with fine mountain scenery in the neighbourhood of Achnashellach Forest. Many of the slopes are covered with firs, thinning out towards higher ground, and ferns and bracken are in great profusion. Loch Doule was at its best, and the trees were showing leaf. A few sheep grazed by the loch side. The railway hid itself with remarkable efficiency, and there was nothing to spoil the beauty of the scene.

The road gradually ascends to more desolate country, giving wild moorland vistas around Loch Scaven and Loch Gowan. This is a bleak windswept district at times, but attractive enough later in the season, when the golden summer breezes have an invigorating quality and there is an airy spaciousness and freedom.

I joined the Gairloch road at Achnasheen near the Station Hotel. One side of the hotel is built on to the railway platform, and there is much bustle and excitement when a train arrives, especially in the evening when the westbound and eastbound expresses on the Kyle-Inverness route meet for a while. Passengers from Kyle who are desolate at the thought of leaving the beauties of Skye thus have a last chance to change trains and return to the charms of the Misty Isle. If you should stay here you may be awakened in the morning by the noise and clatter of an early train, or perhaps by the lowing and stamping of cattle.

As we approach Glen Docherty, passing lonely Loch Rosque, there are grand panoramas of distant and apparently snow-tipped mountains; actually, the white patches are gleaming quartzite catching the rays of the sun. The effect is both striking and bizarre, and lends a unique touch to a landscape comprising the most ancient rock surfaces in the world.

The far north-west, from the Torridon mountains to Cape Wrath, is a happy hunting ground for geologists and a paradise for all lovers of magnificent scenery. If this should be your first visit to these lonely regions, you will surely pause to admire the view of Loch Maree from Glen Docherty— a wonderful view on a clear sunny day, with the incredibly blue waters of Loch Maree extending for miles to the north-west. The loch is perfectly cradled between sweeping hills, dominated to the east by the squat bulk of Slioch, towering to a height of 3260 feet.

The lofty buttresses of Ben Eay come into view as we approach Kinlochewe, but the full beauty of this mountain is best seen from the road to Upper Loch Torridon. The eastern face of the mountain is a glittering mass of white quartzite, and when gleaming in strong sunlight its appearance is quite uncanny. Beyond Loch Clair, a picturesque sheet of water enhanced by a fringe of trees, are the terrific cliffs and precipices of Liathach. Ben Eay and Liathach dominate Glen Torridon, and Liathach is the more spectacular, with its dizzy peaks and pinnacles. Both mountains are very popular with climbers.

The tiny hamlet of Torridon, at the head of Upper Loch Torridon, is in a setting of serene beauty, and across the loch we can see the lonely road from Shieldaig to Loch Damph. An adventurous road leads from Torridon to Inver Alligin, and over the hills to Loch Diabaig. The descent to the tiny hamlet of Lower Diabaig is one of the steepest in Britain. Like so many roads to the western seaboard there is no circular route to the next loch northwards, and in order to reach Gairloch the motorist must return all the way to Kinlochewe, although this is no hardship in such lovely surroundings. Walkers can follow a path from Lower Diabaig around the coast to Red Point and Port Henderson, from where a motoring road leads to Gairloch.

CHAPTER FOURTEEN

LOCH MAREE TO ULLAPOOL

L OCH MAREE is twelve and a half miles in length, and its wooded shores and islets add warmth to a scene which might otherwise be rather desolate, with the slopes of Slioch, composed of Torridon sandstone, towering majestically above. The effect is very impressive, and every detail of its rock face can be seen. Ben Lair, more distantly situated to the north-west, has gentler contours, its lower slopes being thickly wooded. A rough path leads southwards from Bridge of Grudie to Glen Grudie, a track familiar to mountaineers, approaching the majestic corrie between the northern and western spurs of Ben Eay. The 1250-foot cliffs give a far more spectacular view of Ben Eay than can be seen from Kinlochewe or Glen Torridon.

The Loch Maree Hotel at Talladale is a convenient base for exploring the Isles of Maree. Although one of the smaller islands of the loch, Isle Maree is perhaps the most famous, as it was here that St. Maelrubha had his hermitage. St. Maelrubha founded a church at Applecross in 673, from where he visited Kilchrist Church at Strath in Skye. He is said to have founded the ancient chapel, now in ruins, on Isle Maree. 'Maree' is, of course, a corruption of Maelrubha, after whom both island and loch are named. There is a burial-ground on the island, a holy well (now dry), and a tree covered with coins left by pilgrims and visitors. There is also a legend connected with Isle Maree which would serve as an object lesson to young lovers. The story dates from the time of the Norsemen, when a prince of Norway married the daughter of a Celtic chief. During the absence of her husband on an expedition the girl began to doubt whether her husband was still in love with her. So when he returned she pretended to be dead. Upon seeing his wife apparently dead, the distraught husband plunged a dagger into his heart. In a frenzy of remorse and despair the girl seized the dagger from her husband's body and plunged it into her own heart. The tragic couple were buried on

he Cuillin from
ar Drynoch,
inginish

ISLE OF SKYE

nan Gillean
gurr a'
eir from
chan

Dunvegan Castl

ISLE OF SKYE

Idrigil, cliffs o
Bay and Vate
northern Skye

Isle Maree, and commemorated by two slabs facing each other, each bearing an ancient cross.

Beyond Slatadale the Gairloch road leaves the shores of Loch Maree, and after a short distance descends to the coast by way of Kerrysdale. In earlier days this used to be a very beautiful glen, but timber-felling has marred its splendour. The grandeur of its falls, where the River Kerry plunges into a rocky cauldron, still remains. Before entering Flowerdale we can follow the branch road westwards to Shieldaig Lodge, now a comfortable hotel on the verge of Loch Shieldaig. This loch has no connexion with the Loch Shieldaig on the southern shores of Loch Torridon—you will find considerable duplication of place names when exploring the West Highlands. This Loch Shieldaig opens into Gair Loch, not to be confused with the Gare Loch we encountered in Dunbartonshire.

The road continues still further westwards to the small hotel at Badachro, overlooking Eilean Horrisdale and Gairloch itself. This is a very secluded clachan, where a stone jetty, covered with great masses of seaweed, indicates a remarkable rise and fall of the tide. The road ends at Port Henderson, but a track leads southwards to Lower Diabaig on the northern shore of Loch Torridon.

You will like the walk from Gairloch to Flowerdale House, a most attractively situated mansion. Gairloch itself is dominated by an enormous hotel. Boating, fishing and bathing are the main attractions, apart from the surrounding scenery. The sands are among the finest in Scotland, and are at their best on a lazy sunny day, when the waves are gently creeping towards the golden shore and the sea reflects the purest blue from a serene sky. Take an evening walk along the Melvaig road to the oddly-named hamlets of Big and Little Sand, and watch the sunset over Longa Island, and the distant Quiraing of northern Skye.

The route from Gairloch to Dundonnell and Braemore, where the Ullapool road is joined, is one of surpassing beauty. The descent of Gruinard Hill will call for some care, but compared with Mam Rattachan and the Pass of the Cattle you will hardly call it a hill at all. The magnificent mountain scenery, rugged coastline and distant views of seascape and islands are all superb, and I commend this as one of the finest touring routes in the West Highlands.

Beyond Gairloch the road winds between the outcrops of gneiss and descends towards Poolewe, passing a lane leading to Tollie and the landing place at the north-western tip of Loch Maree. If you climb a hill near the roadside you will be rewarded by a splendid view of Loch Maree with its islands, and the entire mountain range from Beinn Airidh Charr to Ben Lair and Slioch. The mouth of the loch is only a mile from this viewpoint, and the scene is as unexpected as it is magnificent.

Loch Maree is separated from the sea at Loch Ewe by the River Ewe, a famous salmon river of considerable width but only three miles long. Poolewe is a quiet, sheltered little village with a very mild climate. There is a hotel and much local fishing. Walkers can work their way round the coast to Rudha Reidh Lighthouse, described by Seton Gordon in *Highways and Byways in the West Highlands*.

The Aultbea road passes Inverewe House and Tournaig, where Osgood Mackenzie, author of *A Hundred Years in the Highlands*, grew many semi-tropical plants and ornamental trees. Inverewe Garden is open to tourists, and thousands visit it every year. The winding and hilly road to Aultbea gives good views of Loch Ewe and the Isle of Ewe, and you can follow a track to the crofts of Mellon Charles.

The peninsula of Rudha Mor separates Gruinard Bay from Loch Ewe, and once this is crossed we come to a fascinating coastline sprinkled with crofts, shielings and strangely named hamlets such as Mellon Idrigil, Laide, Sand, First Coast, Second Coast and Little Gruinard. There are widespread views to Priest Island and the distant Summer Isles, while still more distant mountains to the far north give promise of greater joys to come.

Stay a while near First Coast to see a cluster of crofters' cottages. Many are now in ruins, but even the best appear only slightly superior to the Hebridean 'black-house'. Second Coast is only a few hundred yards away, and this little clachan has its cottages and shielings facing to the east. Some are very primitive indeed, and their thatched roofs are held down by heavy stones tied to ropes as is the practice in Skye. Crofters did not own the primitive dwellings in which they lived but paid rent in the form of labour.

Beyond Second Coast we cross a tumbling stream by a very primitive stone bridge, and soon reach the top of Gruinard Hill, with a breath-taking view of the coast some 300 feet below. Before descending, it is worth climbing a rocky hillock between road and coast to see the view across Little Gruinard Bay to the fantastic peaks of An Teallach. This bay, with its sands and green machair, is exquisitely colourful on a sunny day, when creamy waves break in white cascades of surf on the beach far beneath. If you can tear yourself away from this entrancing viewpoint, descend Gruinard Hill with due caution and halt at the bridge across the Little Gruinard river.

The Little Gruinard river is strewn with huge boulders, which cause sparkling cascades and foam-flecked water. Beautiful though this is, the scene is still more effective a few hundred yards further along, where the road creeps to the edge of a bewitching sandy bay beside a little stream. At times the sand blows over the road, and this sheltered corner of the coast is one of the loveliest scenes on this exquisite journey. The road turns inland for a short distance, crosses the Gruinard river and passes the charmingly situated Gruinard House opposite Gruinard Island, a veritable house in Arcady.

After a steady climb to the top of a promontory, we can pause in amazement at the tremendous panorama eastwards to the head of Little Loch Broom and the lonely mountains of Inverlael Forest. There are mountains everywhere; the hills of Gruinard Forest culminate in the magnificent ridge of An Teallach, and just across Little Loch Broom the twin peaks of Ben Goleach gaze at us in stern isolation. This is a rather frightening view, due to the utter solitude of the scene. The road seems inexpressively forlorn and lonely, and one can see a vast distance without sight of human habitation.

The road is unusually straight for the next seven miles to the head of the sea loch at Dundonnell, but do not miss the rather impressive Ardessie Falls nearby. The small Dundonnell hotel is the only one for many miles around, though a teashop at Camusnagaul, two miles to the west, provides accomodation in the summer, and other nearby houses offer rooms.

There is a rough track from Dundonnell to Aultnaharrie on the south side of Loch Broom, where the walker can be ferried across to Ullapool. This very bad and hilly road is unsuitable for cars.

Beyond Dundonnell the road turns inland and follows a very wild glen passing Dundonnell House and a wooded gorge, which will serve as a fitting introduction to the ravines and canyons with which this district abounds. I have approached this ravine from several points, but the booming of water was the only indication of its great depth. The road climbs steadily until the ravine and trees are left far behind, and we encounter steep moorland with a cascading stream on one side, forming a fine series of waterfalls. The highest point is reached at a height of 1110 feet on the desolate plateau of Dundonnell Forest. There are now wonderful views of the imposing An Teallach ridge, whose jagged peaks and serrated edges echo something of the grim quality of the Cuillin. The road across this bleak moor is straight and lonely for several miles, and must nearly break the heart of a pedestrian—for this is a cheerless and inhospitable route. Apart from Teallach there is nothing but a wilderness of desolate moor and bog. The road is called 'Destitution Road', not as an apt title to describe its barren appearance, but because it was first made to provide work for the surrounding communities when they came near to starving during the potato famine of a century ago.

The road descends to Glen More, and we come to a most sinister region forming a trap for the unwary. If you should leave the wayside I advise you to tread with the greatest caution. After crossing the stream the road is still some 600 feet above sea level, and continues high above a wooded gorge. But the stream descends deeper and deeper into the ravine and can only be seen with difficulty. When it is seen, a hundred or more feet below, it reveals sullen froth winking and bubbling in ghastly derision. Horrible as it is, this gorge is less fearsome than Corriehalloch, which we approach as the road turns eastwards towards Braemore Lodge. There is, however, a wonderful view of Strath More and the distant beauty of Loch Broom. The road is high above the deep gash of Corriehalloch, now shrouded in greenery.

It is only a few hundred yards to the Ullapool road at Braemore Lodge, and we soon reach the opposite side of the gorge to find a path leading to Corriehalloch, which means 'Filthy Hollow'. The track is approached through a small gate at the roadside, and this track can be a little dangerous in wet weather, when it becomes very slippery. Once on the small foot-bridge I think even the most hardened sightseer would pause aghast. You look down a sheer canyon with crumbling cliffs, and the surging river is

Quiraing and
maluag Bay,
tternish

ISLE OF SKYE AND THE OUTER HEBRIDES

Outer Hebrides
near Kilvaxter,
ern Skye

ISLE OF SKYE

Duntulm Castl
Duntulm Lodg
and Fladda C
from Duntulm
Outer Hebride
on the horizon

228 feet beneath. On the other side of the bridge the river is almost at eye level and plunges into the awful depths below, thus forming the famous Falls of Measach. There is not much water in dry weather, but in time of flood there is more than enough, and the canyon becomes filled with spray. At such times satellite streams add their quota to the fearsome scene, and spill over into the dark abyss to add further confusion to the tortured waters beneath. When you have seen all this you will treat the narrow path along the crumbling edge of the canyon with the respect that it deserves!

V. Carron Wellington vividly describes, in *The Adventures of a Sporting Angler* how he made his way up the canyon and fished the river near the foot of the falls. His account gives a remarkable impression of the horror of this sinister spot.

The precipitous cliffs of Corriehalloch are the home of many ferns and mosses which receive ample moisture from the swirling clouds of spray, and even in dry weather this ravine is cold and dank. I first visited the place in August 1934 and could not have chosen a better time, as I encountered a party busy measuring the drop with an immensely long rope marked in yard lengths. The exact drop, from the bridge to the water, was found to be 228 feet, and the water was eighteen feet in depth. You can see what appears to be a matchstalk at the foot of the ravine. Actually it is a huge larch log once hauled by a horse along the edge of the abyss. The brink of the north side of the chasm suddenly crumbled away, taking with it horse and log.

The road descends to Inverlael, and you can obtain a glimpse of Corriehalloch from the roadside, although you will not see the bottom. Timber-felling operations have lessened the beauty of Strath More, but the road ahead to Ullapool offers grand views of Loch Broom and the rows of neat white houses on Ullapool Point. Perhaps the best view of the village is from the Braes of Ullapool, easily reached from the Loch Broom road just before the descent into Ullapool.

Ullapool is as distinctive in its way as Inveraray, and a curious feature is the precise way in which the neat whitewashed houses are set out. No doubt this remarkable town-planning can be attributed to the British Fisheries Association who established the village in 1788, hoping to revive the herring industry. Although still a fishing village it is now increasing in favour as a tourist resort, and is very popular with anglers. I remember once sitting on a bollard at the end of the harbour and admiring the trim white houses set well back above the sloping beach. Despite a heavy wind and approaching storm-clouds the scene was impressive in its rugged simplicity. It suddenly crossed my mind that I had never seen anything of the wild tract of land stretching for many a mile inland and eastwards. If you look at a map you will be surprised at the complete absence of roads between Ullapool on the west and the Cromarty and Dornoch Firths to the east. This tremendous tract of deer-forest comprises the bulk of Easter Ross.

I decided to walk to Loch Achall some three miles to the east, reached by a track only shown by the vaguest of dotted lines even on the one-inch map, although it is just passable for cars. It seemed a long three miles as I trudged alongside the Ullapool river. The weather became very threatening, and it seemed doubtful if I should reach the loch before nightfall. Despite the proximity of Ullapool I have rarely experienced such overwhelming solitude, and when at last the loch was reached and I saw the desolate view across an interminable stretch of bog and moor towards the heart of Easter Ross, I felt very glad of the security of the track. Apart from a few anglers and local keepers, very few people have ever heard of this lonely sheet of water, and if you would seek complete solitude you will find it here.

CHAPTER FIFTEEN

ULLAPOOL TO UNAPOOL

THERE are unusual features about the view back to Ullapool and Loch Broom from the top of the hill at Morefield. In wet weather there is a feeling of leaving one of the more remote outposts of civilisation. I have experienced much the same feeling in Nova Scotia and in north-west Iceland.

Normally Ullapool enjoys a mild climate, but when it is cold and squally the scene has a very northern quality when one sees bleak inhospitable hills cradling a long, sprawling sea-loch. With a sprinkling of snow and ice the scene might be an Icelandic fjord.

Although parts of the northbound road from Ullapool enjoy an 'A' category, it is an adventurous route which may prove disconcerting to motorists familiar with southern roads. But so long as you are willing to drive slowly (and in no other way can you enjoy the scenery) most of the roads from Ullapool to the far north-west are reasonably good.

You may possibly leave Ullapool on a sparkling morning of sunshine and breeze. On such a morning all my comparisons with more Arctic scenes will vanish like a puff of smoke, and you will see a beauty of colouring and form which I have not seen excelled by the Mediterranean. The character of north-west Highland weather is full of unexpected surprises. I have known the most wretched morning of gale and rain change before lunch into a day of brilliant sun and colourful views. Sunshine after rain always produces rich colouring, but never more so than in the Highlands. At times there is a rich luminosity in which the colours seem to glow and pulsate with life. This strange quality is one of the more elusive charms of the far north-west, and is never forgotten.

The northbound road is impressive from the start, being dominated by Ben More Coigach, which rises abruptly from the sea. The road is very winding and enterprising, giving a succession of grand views culminating in the exquisite scene from the descent to Ardmair beach, opposite Martin Isle and the formidable crags of Ben More Coigach. The shore at this point forms a gracefully curved bay shelving steeply to the sea, and is separated from the road by a narrow strip of green machair. The beach is resplendent with innumerable gleaming white pebbles and curved lines of seaweed.

A short distance beyond Ardmair the road climbs to higher ground, giving further delightful views looking back towards the curious spit of land forming the northern tip of Ardmair Bay. Beyond this the squat shape of Ben Goleach is unmistakable, and there are seaward views towards the Summer Isles. The road leaves this delightful coast and turns inland, giving sombre views of the distant mountains to the north-west. The view eastwards towards the Rhidorroch Forest is a wilderness of bog, moorlands and lochans.

Beyond Drumrunie Lodge (now a hotel), we come to an important road junction. There are not many roads in this part of the world, and a road junction is a matter of some consequence. If you will turn to a map you will see that both roads go to Lochinver. The road to the west reaches the coast at Enard Bay, and is the nearer and more attractive route. The other route is longer but quicker, as it is a much better road, and at Ledmore joins the main road from Bonar Bridge, continuing to Inchnadamph and Loch Assynt.

North of Inchnadamph the road continues to the Kylesku Ferry, joined near Unapool by the coast road from Lochinver to Stoer and Eddrachillis Bay. All these roads are worth visiting, and it is a matter of some nicety planning how best to visit them all. Much will depend upon the weather and the time at your disposal. The best plan is to use Lochinver as a base for two circular tours, which will cover all the roads with the minimum of trouble and give adequate time for a fairly leisurely appreciation of the truly superb scenery.

The finer route is along the coast from Enard Bay to Lochinver, Stoer, Drumbeg, Unapool and Kylesku. So we turn westwards beyond Drumrunie, and descend to lonely Loch Lurgain, with Cul Beag rising almost from the roadside.

The most remarkable feature of the landscape is Stack Polly. If you can imagine a petrified hedgehog 2009 feet in height, you will have an excellent idea of Stack Polly. This remarkable hill is composed of red Torridonian sandstone with no protective covering of quartzite, and its strange shape is due to the weather having eroded the rock into bristling pinnacles. Like other strange mountains in this district, such as Suilven, Stack Polly appears cone-shaped from the west, and its serrated outline is best seen from the Loch Lurgain road to the south.

Loch Badagyle is almost a continuation of Loch Lurgain to the west, and it is tempting to continue to Polbain and Achiltibuie, where you will find a hotel and a wonderful view of the Summer Isles, the largest of which is Tanera More.

Readers of Dr Fraser Darling's *Island Farm* will remember that this was the island which he converted from an unproductive wilderness to useful farm-land. The value of such a remarkable achievement is obvious, and shows that with the right leadership farming can be a productive and paying pro-position, even under the most adverse conditions prevailing in the loneliest and most remote corners of the western seaboard. The National Trust for Scotland possess an equally remote property at Burg on the west coast of Mull. This, too, was little more than a decaying bracken-strewn wilderness when the Trust took it over, but is now a flourishing farm. So there is hope for the more remote regions of the Highlands, and the secret lies in modern farming methods and the right type of leadership.

The road from Badnagyle to Lochinver is quite fascinating, and you will need a keen sense of direction to identify your surroundings. This is a very narrow, hilly and tortuous route, and the best that can be said of the road surface is that it is passable. To tourists unused to roads of this type I can only urge that the scenic compensations far outweigh the driving difficulties, and that most of the latter will completely disappear if a car is driven at a mere crawl.

The whole district is a maze of indented coastline, short sea lochs and myriads of tiny inland lochans, often satellites of some larger fresh-water loch. Some of the biggest lochs are dotted with islets. There seems to be more water than land, and much of the land consists of rocky outcrops of primeval gneiss or bracken-covered slopes with intervening patches of bog and swamp. This strange scene is overlooked by a number of mountains of the weirdest and most unearthly aspect.

We have already noticed Stack Polly, but Cul Mor, Cul Beag, Suilven and Canisp all have this fantastic appearance. Suilven, in particular, when seen from the west, presents an almost sheer wall of rock rising in the form of a perfect cone, hence its other name, the Sugar Loaf. Due to the continual twisting of the road Suilven keeps turning up in the most unexpected places, and at times you may feel you are on the wrong road. But there is only one place where it is possible to go wrong, and that is immediately after crossing the River Polly, where you may be inclined to follow a track northwards to Inverpolly and the coast instead of turning inland. Our route does eventually wind round to the coast, reaching it at the north-west corner of Enard Bay. Once, when scrambling around this district, I selected a rocky viewpoint and sat down, not noticing that I was sharing the rock with a large, coiled adder. It lay basking in the sun and blended so perfectly with the rock that I did not see it for several minutes. It was a good thing my quiet companion had no dislike for strangers!

There is a steep descent to Inverkirkaig, a sheltered and wooded spot of great natural beauty. Once across the bridge over the swiftly-coursing River Kirkaig, we are in Sutherland, seen at its best along the coast from Inverkirkaig to Cape Wrath, the wildest, most completely unspoiled and loneliest part of the British mainland. It is also the grandest, and although we have enjoyed many lovely scenes during the earlier stages of our journey, it is only right that the most exquisite scenes of all should be reserved for our wanderings through the 'fairy lands forlorn' of north-western Sutherland.

It is not far from Inverkirkaig to Strathan and Lochinver, but every yard is full of beauty. The landscape largely consists of outcrops of Lewisian gneiss forming rocky hills. The coastline is very indented, and occasional crofts and whitewashed houses blend harmoniously with the landscape. A few trees, a few grass patches and delicately coloured seaweed add colour to the scene, and the journey to Lochinver seems all too short.

Lochinver is an ideal place for a fishing holiday, as there are at least 280 tiny lochans in the parish, and first-class sea fishing and salmon fishing in the rivers Inver and Kirkaig. A good harbour, pier, and convenient anchorage provide for yachts and pleasure steamers. The climber, naturalist, botanist and tourist will find this an entrancing district.

The strange peaks of Cul Mor, Suilven and Canisp dominate the surroundings, but are much farther away than they seem, and can only be reached by a rough tramp across the intervening wastes of bog, swamp and tiny lochans. Suilven in particular is difficult of access, and its tremendous west face gives some climbing of considerable difficulty and exposure. The weak links in its armour consist of extremely steep vegetatious gullies. There are many short walks in the neighbourhood, and the lonely crofts of Badinaban, Baddidarroch and Achmelvich are worth visiting. The best walk of all is from Inverkirkaig to the Falls of Kirkaig, which have a drop of sixty feet. The return walk from Inverkirkaig is about five miles.

We can make two excellent circular tours from Lochinver. The easier but slightly less attractive route involves a drive of about fifty miles to Loch Assynt, Elphin and Enard Bay. There is little of note for the first few miles except distant views of Suilven and Canisp. But there are other mountains to notice as we drive eastwards. The peaks of Quinag are the most northerly, and are separated from the rounded bulk of Glasven by the bleak pass which carries the northbound road to Unapool and Kylesku Ferry. Further to the south-east is Ben More Assynt, in whose grim fastness lies the source of the River Oykell. This mountain, the highest in Sutherland, is largely composed of quartzite, and the usual route to the top involves the preliminary ascent of the subsidiary peak of Conaveall, only nineteen feet lower than the main peak.

The scenery improves as we approach Loch Assynt Lodge. The trees and ferns do much to mitigate the bleakness of the surroundings. Loch Assynt is about seven miles in length, and as we approach Skiag Bridge we pass the junction of the northbound road to Kylesku Ferry. Shortly beyond this point are the ruins of Ardvreck Castle, built in the fifteenth century, and for long a stronghold of the Macleods of Assynt. The castle is on a narrow promontory, a notable landmark on the shores of the loch, and is approached by a slender isthmus. It is worth looking over the few remaining traces of the castle, which is only a short walk from the roadside. Like so many other Scottish castles, it is a place of sad and bitter memories.

It was here that the great Montrose is said to have been betrayed by a Macleod of Assynt. After the Marquis of Montrose was defeated at Carbisdale in 1650, a sad sequel to his great victory at Inverlochy Castle in 1645, he fled towards Assynt with two companions. Wild though this district now is, it must have been much more inhospitable over 300 years ago, and there would be few roads, if any. The three fugitives were compelled to separate, and as there was a huge reward for Montrose it was not long before he was captured. He is said to have been found by a servant of Neil Macleod of Assynt, and taken to Ardvreck Castle in a half-starved condition. He was imprisoned at the castle for a time and then taken to Edinburgh, being led on horseback while suffering from high fever as a result of exposure and hardship. Although in a sad and pitiable condition he preserved the utmost fortitude and courage to the end. His composure at the time of his execution won the admiration of the crowds who had come to abuse and jeer.

Montrose was not so fortunate as Prince Charlie. The sum of £30,000 was offered for the capture of the Prince, a tremendous sum at that period, but not one of the meanest and poorest of his subjects sought to betray him, and they had many opportunities to do so. Montrose was betrayed for £20,000 in cash and a large quantity of oatmeal. It seems that retribution overtook Neil Macleod. He was subsequently declared a rebel, and the estate of Assynt passed to the MacKenzies, who built the seventeenth century Calda House, the ruins of which may still be seen near Ardvreck Castle.

We continue south through bleak country between Canisp and Breabeg, only relieved by limestone cliffs near Stronechrubie and the island-studded Loch Awe. Turning westwards near Ledmore Lodge we follow the Ullapool road to Cam Loch and Elphin, an exposed and rather scattered clachan as unusual as its name. There is a sad little cemetery here, overlooking a grim and uninviting landscape with Loch Vevatie and Cam Loch in the foreground, and Canisp and the Ben More Assynt massif in the background. You will see little else at Elphin beyond a few cottages, scattered crofts, a post office and a school, and yet there is some elusive quality about this lonely and exposed little township which has caused me to stop again and again.

The road now climbs to the base of a forbidding scree-covered crag, an

Crofter's cottage
Carbost

ISLE OF SKYE

Isle of Rum
from Elgol,
Southern Skye

Allt a' Mhuill
and north fa
of Ben Nevis

BEN NEVIS AND LOCH NEVIS, INVERNESS-SHIRE

Loch Nevis
from the beac
at Mallaigvaig

outlying spur of the Cromalt Hills. It is worth stopping to look back at the strangely enthralling view. On a sunny day the imposing spur of the Cromalt Hills lights up with an effect of limestone rather than quartzite, and the lonely road is seen descending to Elphin against a tremendous background of grim majestic mountains. Resuming our journey we cross rather bleak and uninteresting moorland, only relieved from monotony by the dominating shapes of Cul Mor and Cul Beag. Just beyond Drumrunie Old Lodge we reach the road junction, and return to Lochinver by the Enard Bay and Inverkirkaig route previously described.

The second and more adventurous circular tour from Lochinver covers a distance of about forty-five miles, and is not a journey I recommend in bad weather. Although the road to Stoer, Drumbeg and Unapool is the next stage on our tour of the western seaboard, the route can easily be converted into a circular tour by following the road from Unapool to Loch Assynt, and returning westwards to Lochinver. It will thus be seen that there are two ways to Unapool from Lochinver. The easier, shorter and much less interesting route is to follow the main road to Loch Assynt and Skiag Bridge, from where a narrow and difficult hill road negotiates a desolate pass between Quinag and Glasven.

There are bleak views from the top. To the north is a prospect as grim and forbidding as any in Scotland. You will see nothing but trackless wastes of peat-bogs and moor, disappearing towards a land of remote hills and deer forests. Quinag, to the west, presents a sphinx-like face, and should you look east you will recoil from the grim cold outline of Glasven, guarding the chill, unfriendly waters of Loch Ganvich. Should you stop for a while there will be no sound but the distant rumble of waterfalls descending to the shores of Loch Glendhu and Loch Glencoul. One of the highest waterfalls in Scotland descends 300 feet to the head of Loch Glencoul. It is seven miles from Skiag Bridge to Unapool, and this is the usual route to Kylesku Ferry and the north.

The coast road from Lochinver to Drumbeg and Unapool is far more picturesque, although the last six miles are quite adventurous, involving several short but steep hills over a very narrow track with a poor surface. If you have followed our route as far as this you will have no trouble with the Drumbeg to Unapool route. The enthusiastic driver will find that this road offers wide scope for all the niceties of skilled driving, and is even more lovely than the road from Enard Bay to Lochinver. If I were asked to select the most beautiful coast road on the whole of the western seaboard, this would be my choice.

Sutherland was at its best the day I left Lochinver and headed for Stoer. It was one of those intensely clear, sunny days following a period of rain. Fleecy clouds, a light breeze and a sparkle and brilliance of colouring made the journey a sheer delight. I was also filled with the spirit of adventure as this was the first time I had ever had the opportunity to follow the entire route from Stoer to Unapool.

The Stoer road leaves the Loch Assynt road a short distance beyond Lochinver, and climbs a rocky brae to the west. Stop at the top and look back to the silent sentinels of Sutherland—Canisp, Suilven, Cul Mor, Cul Beag and Stack Polly. Strangely enough the quintet are evenly spaced, and form a most orderly pattern in great contrast to the way they appeared, one at a time, like shrouded ghosts on our approach to Lochinver from the south. They have often been likened to mountains of the moon, probably because we have nothing quite like them anywhere else.

The road dips to the sea at the very narrow head of Loch Roe, but soon leaves it again to wind uneasily through a labyrinth of outcrops of gneiss and small reed-fringed lochans, until quite suddenly it descends towards Stoer Bay, distinguished by a patch of dazzling white sand, whiter even than the sands of Morar.

The beauty of Stoer Bay lies in the broad expanse of smooth, dazzling white sands. The sea was the purest blue in colour, and had that clarity noticeable at Iona. Great breakers were rushing towards the shore to fall in a riot of creamy spume, fascinating to watch. It was possible to follow in the wake of a receding wave some twenty or thirty feet before the next surging monster came rushing up. I climbed along the line of rocks leading seawards, and watched the waves as they rushed past. One, bigger than the rest, burst on my rocky viewpoint, enveloping me in a cloud of spray. I cautiously crawled back to the beach, and soon dried in the hot sun. I could cheerfully have spent the rest of the day in this delightful spot, and lingered so long that I had not time to follow the track out to Stoerhead lighthouse and walk to the Point of Stoer.

The Drumbeg road crosses drifts of sand blown inland from Stoer Bay, surmounts the peninsula of Rhu Stoer, and then creeps along the cliffs of Clashnessie Bay. This is a typical Sutherland road, engineered with great ingenuity and held together by deep stone embankments descending sheer to the sea. Traffic is very infrequent, and I did not meet a single car during the entire journey.

This is a heavenly route, and you will see alluring views towards remote rocky headlands. The colouring of sea, turf, sands, machair and rock baffle description, and I can only hope that you may come this way in fine weather. The stony shores of the inland Loch Drumbeg introduce an unusual view of Quinag, which gradually dominates the landscape as we continue eastwards. Occasional glimpses to the north reveal the myriad islets of Eddrachillis Bay, and the sheer cliffs of Handa Isle nine miles distant.

Drumbeg is a scattered clachan with a small hotel. Beyond Drumbeg the road degenerates into a sandy track barely car-width, with several hills. Although the steepest gradient is no more than 1 in 5, the surface is loose, and some care will be needed to avoid wheelspin, especially on the acute bends. So long as this route is driven very slowly and steadily it is quite passable, and the surface is not bad enough to damage the car.

Just beyond Drumbeg there is a most majestic view of Quinag. The road then descends steeply to the lonely clachan of Nedd above the wooded shores of Loch Nedd, and reaches sea level at the bridge across the stream flowing from Glenleraig. The track then makes a long and steep ascent over bleak moorland, descending just as steeply towards Loch Ardvar. This is followed by a tricky ascent and descent to Glen Ardvar nearly at sea level. We then have another long winding ascent to Loch Cairnbawn, and the worst is over. It is interesting to stop at the various high points on this switch-back route and look back at the extensive views, each characterised by the zig-zag course of the track as it tortuously negotiates the various hills. It is magnificent and adventurous motoring, but your car should be nursed very carefully over this route.

The track keeps high above Loch Cairnbawn, giving wild views across to Kylestrome. The lonely cottage at Torgawn near the shore of the loch is in an almost idyllic situation. The track, now extremely narrow, descends to the Allt a' Ghamhna and then climbs on to open moorland directly opposite Sail Ghorm and Sail Gharbh, the northern spurs of Quinag.

Some years ago I climbed Quinag with two friends, on a rather cold and misty autumn afternoon. The walk from Torgawn and back was just seven miles, which we accomplished in precisely five hours. Apart from a short halt at the summit we did not stop anywhere, and the time was mostly spent in surmounting the difficulties of the intervening terrain rather than conquering the mountain itself.

We crossed half a mile of rough, peaty moorland, fortunately not very boggy due to a preceding dry season, and came to the Allt a' Ghamhna, a fairly wide stream which held us up quite a time. After prowling along the banks we eventually found a place where we could risk a flying leap. We crossed the Allt a' Bhathaich, which flowed from the wide corrie separating Sail Ghorm from Sail Gharbh, and then climbed into the corrie, keeping to the eastern shoulder of Sail Gharbh. Beyond the corrie the angle steepened, and we scrambled up steep grass and scree slopes to the summit ridge.

Like so many Scottish ridges, there is nothing to see until you reach the top, and then the view bursts with breath-taking impact, generally attended by a fierce and unexpected wind. We had been protected from the westerly wind during the ascent, but as soon as we reached the ridge it hurled itself against us with great force, giving little chance to study the view until we had wedged ourselves securely against convenient rocks.

There was considerable snow on the summit and the view was magnificent in its desolate splendour. Loch Assynt was directly beneath, and we looked down on to the summit of Suilven, which seemed much nearer than seven miles. Canisp, some six miles away, looked very imposing, its summit being slightly higher than our viewpoint. Visibility did not extend beyond Enard Bay and Rhu Coigach, but we had ample opportunity to study the myriads of lochs dotting the surface of the bleak moorland far below. It was a grim and inhospitable wilderness, and my gaze turned towards Lochinver with something like nostalgia. To the east we could see across Loch Glencoul to Bed Leoid, with Glas Bheinn and Ben More Assynt further to the south.

Loch Kishorn from
the Bealach na Ba
(Pass of the Cattle)
at sunset

ROSS AND CROMARTY

Loch Maree from
Glen Docherty

Glen Carron ne
Achnashellach
Forest

ROSS AND CROMARTY

Gruinard Bay
An Teallach fr
Gruinard Hill,
Wester Ross

The wisp of road between Skiag Bridge and Unapool looked sad and dejected in its solitude.

In very clear weather the view to the north should extend to Cape Wrath itself, but on this occasion I could see little beyond Ben Stack and Ben Arkle, although Foinaven was just recognisable as a rather indistinct blur. The best view of all was to the west, revealing the beauty of Eddrachillis Bay and the Point of Stoer.

It was very cold on top, and we did not stay longer than ten minutes. I picked up a pebble of quartzite as a souvenir of our visit, and then descended into the shelter of the deep corrie from which we had climbed. Seasoned mountaineers would laugh long and joyously at my method of descending precipitous grass slopes. After anxiously locating the least horrible gully, I lie flat on my back and, peering at the drop beneath my feet, cautiously slide down a few inches at a time, carefully steering for any slight excrescences of rock to stem any chance of too rapid progress. But Quinag was in genial mood, and treated me with stony justice.

A spell of scrambling among huge boulders and wading through burns was followed by a brisk return along the road to Torgawn, and so ended a rather hectic expedition compressed into five hours.

Now that I had driven to within sight of the great corrie between Sail Ghorm and Sail Gharbh I viewed the scene with something like affection. But this time I came alone, and the scene seemed much lonelier. The grimmest desolation is often relieved by a cheerful companion.

I continued to Loch Unapool, and shortly afterwards joined the road from Skiag Bridge. This will be your way back to Lochinver if you are treating the present portion of our route as a circular tour. But my course lay northwards, and I descended to Loch Glencoul and the lonely clachan of Unapool, where I found Kylesku post office. This must be one of the loneliest post offices in Britain, and it enjoys a commanding situation overlooking the trackless shores of Loch Glencoul, dominated by the strangely shaped peak of Ben Leoid. Soon afterwards I reached the cosy Kylesku Hotel near the ferry.

CHAPTER SIXTEEN

KYLESKU TO KINLOCHBERVIE

KYLESKU occupies one of the strangest and most impressive situations in the far north-west. The small hotel is built at the tip of a promontory facing another narrow promontory, which juts from Kylestrome on the northern shore of Loch Cairnbawn.

Several islands, of which Garbh Eilean is the largest, add to this odd mixture of land and water. The sea-loch to the west of the ferry is Loch Cairnbawn, giving access to two remote sea-lochs to the east and south-east of Kylesku. These latter sea-arms, Lochs Glendhu and Glencoul, penetrate some of the most awesome and inaccessible regions in Britain. Majestic mountains rise abruptly from rugged shores, and tremendous waterfalls thunder down from the heights above. Their remote fastnesses are presided over by Quinag, Glas Bheinn and Ben Leoid, and it would be hard to find a more awesome trio anywhere on the Scottish mainland.

The scene can be beautiful by the soft, mellow light of the harvest moon. I remember a warm still evening with scarcely a breath of wind, and no sound beyond the distant tinkle of falling water from the lonely waterfalls so prolific in this district. I could see Quinag in surprising detail, and even the grim outline of Ben Leoid was softened by the moonlight. There was a haunting magic and wistful sadness about the scene which I have never forgotten.

As I left Kylesku a westerly gale was approaching. It is surprising how soon a westerly gale can turn the loveliest day into a turmoil of squalls and tempest. The two promontories on either shore are quite near, but the intervening strip of water was already ruffled into choppy waves by the approaching gale, and the current was brisk and purposeful. I expected to pay 10/- for the crossing, and was amazed to learn that this is now a free ferry, and there was no charge at all! This ferry avoids a detour of 100 miles, and runs on Sundays as well as weekdays.

I was left on the narrow neck of land at Kylestrome, from where there is an impressive view of Quinag, but I must admit to feeling indescribably lonely. The northbound road is shown on the maps as an 'A' road. If it were in England it would warrant description as an unclassified cart track. It is wider than the road from Drumbeg to Unapool and not quite as hilly, but I found the surface execrable and full of pot-holes on the long ten miles to Scourie. If there is any chance of a sunset and you can follow this route in the evening, you will never forget the gorgeous colouring and seascapes towards the myriad tiny islets of Eddrachillis Bay and the distant Outer Hebrides.

This adventurous road turns inland beyond Kylestrome Lodge and twists and turns through typical Sutherland scenery. Duartmore Bridge is crossed at the head of an extremely narrow loch, narrower than many rivers, but it is at Calva Bay that the views from the road become superb. Between Calva Bay and Badcall there are sublime views across Eddrachillis Bay, with its host of rocky islets, to the coastline of north Lewis.

I remember once seeing an exquisite sunset here, and its beauty has haunted me ever since. I shall never forget how the incredible blue of the sea melted into the golden reflections of the sunset. There were broken clouds which seemed almost molten. I sat on the turf beside the grey rocks of Eddrachillis, and inhaled the scent of peat and the tang of seaweed. The colouring increased in splendour, and there was an all-pervading hush and stillness, broken only by the occasional sound of a tiny wave, scarcely a ripple, as it fell on the rocky beach.

Handa Isle is the favourite excursion from Scourie, and I once tried to see this mysterious island at dusk. I crossed Scourie Bay, wended my way through some fields, climbed a wall and plunged into a wilderness of tumbling rocks and cliffs. At length I reached the top of the highest hill in the neighbourhood, and saw Handa—a dim uncanny shape in the dusk, with low-lying shores across the Sound of Handa. I could see the slopes rising steeply to the great cliffs to the north and west of the island, and could even see the Outer Hebrides, the atmosphere having a strange translucent quality. So long as there was any light at all, visibility seemed unlimited.

A better way to see Handa is to sail round it in a boat and inspect its sheer cliffs of red Torridonian sandstone, rising from the sea to a height of 400 feet. The island is preserved as a bird sanctuary, and in the breeding season (May to July) bird lovers can watch myriads of puffins, razorbills, guillemots and other sea-fowl. An exhaustive account of the bird life of Handa is given by Robert Atkinson in his book *Island Going*. Although it is impossible to land at the base of these grim cliffs, the island slopes inland to a low eastern shore, which is very sheltered and offers good landing places. There are white sands and a colourful machair.

Handa is no longer inhabited. The last inhabitants left over a century ago to emigrate to America, due to the potato famine of 1845, a catastrophe which brought disaster to the far north-west. There was once a Queen of Handa. The small community used to elect the oldest widow to be their queen, and no doubt, whenever they held meetings in the nature of folk moots, her decision would be final. She was recognised as Queen of Handa not only on the island but on the mainland as well. It must have been a very Spartan community. They lived on fish, potatoes and gulls' eggs, the latter precariously procured by the daring of the island cragsmen. They lived in very primitive dwellings of which little trace remains, and the only remaining building on the island is a solitary shieling, though the graveyard is still in existence. Otherwise Handa is given over to the birds, who doubtless had it first.

The main road, such as it is, turns eastwards beyond Scourie and follows the rocky shores of Loch a Bhaid Daraich beneath the slopes of a beetling cliff. There is a short but steep climb followed by a rather bleak drive through loch-strewn country, surrounded by the usual wilderness of gneiss hills. There is some improvement in the scene as we reach Loch Laxford and Laxford Bay and river. We join the main road from Lairg at Laxford Bridge, and, as the Lairg to Durness road has been reconstructed, it comes as a big surprise to leave the very indifferent Scourie road and join a fast main road with an excellent surface.

Do not expect to find a thriving village at Laxford Bridge. In reality there is a lonely bridge crossing the River Laxford, with no habitation of any kind. The nearest accommodation is at Rhiconich, and even this is a recent development.

73

*eling at Second
st near Little
inard*

WESTER ROSS

*eallach and
ution Road*

74

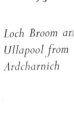

*Loch Broom and
Ullapool from
Ardcharnich*

ROSS AND CROMARTY—SUTHERLAND

Lochinver

It is interesting to note with what ease most of the villages of the far north-west can now be reached. A series of roads radiate from Inverness like spokes from a wheel, and there are direct routes to Kyle of Lochalsh, Gairloch, Ullapool, Lochinver, Scourie, Durness and Tongue. It is only when we want to follow the rim of the wheel, as represented by the western seaboard, that the way becomes complicated. Most of the places we have reached with such difficulty are readily accessible from Inverness by direct routes, hence, however far north you may follow the western seaboard, it is always possible to find a direct and speedy route to the south.

Laxford Bridge is an important junction, and as you stand on the rocky knoll behind the bridge and admire the graceful sweep of the river wending its way to the south-east, the thin line of the Lairg road can be seen starting on its lonely journey towards civilisation. The first twenty-one miles of the route cover most imposing scenery as the road winds alongside the shores of Loch Stack between Ben Stack and Ben Arkle, and continues beside Loch More with the remote mountains of the Reay Forest to the north. This is a very lonely route, but nowhere more so than between Loch Merkland and the Overscaig Hotel. The final sixteen miles to Lairg are alongside the dreary, treeless and monotonous Loch Shin. A fast main road leads from Lairg to Inverness, and the distance of sixty-two miles is soon covered. For those who must return to the south, the Great North Road from Inverness to Perth, Edinburgh and London offers the fastest long distance travel possible on British roads.

Having thus secured our retreat, we may consider the last lap of our journey towards Cape Wrath. For the first five miles we follow the Durness road to Rhiconich, and it feels quite strange to drive along such an excellent road in such a remote corner of Scotland. You will probably have a feeling of relief if you have approached from Kylesku! There are impressive views of Foinaven dominating a foreground composed of several lochans, some reed-fringed and others just bare sullen pools.

At Rhiconich, we reach a road junction at the head of Loch Inchard. This is the start of the last motoring road to the far north-west, and it will take us to the nearest point to Cape Wrath reachable by car. If accommodation has not already been arranged you have the choice of six places in the neighbourhood. The first two are at Rhiconich, the next is at Kinlochbervie five miles distant, and directly on our route. If these should fail there is the Cape Wrath Hotel at Keoldale, thirteen miles to the north, and a mile further, at Durness, are two private hotels.

The road from Rhiconich to Kinlochbervie keeps high above Loch Inchard until the descent to Achriesgill, and it is well to keep a watchful eye on the unguarded drops from the roadside.

A further climb over a promontory between Achriesgill and Badcall gives charming glimpses of scattered crofts, but soon the road appears to descend like a water chute into Loch Innis na Ba Bhuidhe, near Kinlochbervie. A sharp left-hand bend just averts a too close acquaintance with this inland loch, and we climb once again, this time reaching our destination.

The Garbet Hotel enjoys a magnificent view due to its commanding situation high above Kinlochbervie, with Loch na Claise, an alluring sea-loch hardly more than a bay, to the west, Loch Inchard to the south, and Loch Innis na Ba Buidhe to the east. Translated, the name of this last loch signifies 'the loch by which the yellow herd graze', named after a famous herd of golden cattle, the steading of which was once in this vicinity.

The Kinlochbervie estate occupies some fifty square miles containing over a hundred lochs, more than sixty being good for fishing. The estate extends from Sandwood in the north-west to Laxford Bay in the south-west, and to the north-western summit of Foinaven, haunt of the golden eagle and raven. The best centre for this fascinating neighbourhood is undoubtedly Kinlochbervie. There is excellent salmon fishing in the vicinity, as well as brown trout and sea-trout fishing.

Kinlochbervie is now a 'specified port'. A new pier has been built, and already there have been very gratifying landings of herrings and white fish. The approach road we followed from Rhiconich is now greatly improved. The first part of the journey is over a tarred surface, and the remainder of the road has been widened and the surface improved. Part of the cost of this road reconstruction was found by the crofters and residents themselves. There are plans for a water scheme to bring a pipeline to Kinlochbervie. All this industry and activity is having a beneficial effect and bringing new life to one of the most remote villages in Britain.

From the tourist viewpoint Kinlochbervie offers access to some of the finest scenery in Scotland. There are superb views from the village looking back to Loch Inchard, and the tremendous panorama of rolling mountains of Sutherland and Wester Ross. They are all there, including Foinaven, Meall Horn, Ben Arkle and Ben Stack—and in time you will come to recognise them as old friends. There seems no limit to the distance one can see, and it is all completely unspoiled, wild and beautiful country. As a Utopian retreat from the worries and cares of congested city life, Kinlochbervie is a sheer tonic.

The weather has great scope to produce unusual effects over such a broad canvas. I remember gazing from an outcrop of rock above the village one dull evening. The sullen, grey waters of the Loch of the Yellow Herd lay below, and I could see the road curving downwards towards the still surface of the loch. It was nearly dusk, dark clouds were stealing towards the distant mountains, and a profound silence heralded the approach of night. Suddenly a shaft of rich golden light came down from the sky and burned with a strange glow over the glass-like waters of the loch. The surrounding crags were transformed into glorious bastions of creamy marble and graced the golden beauty of the loch, making a picture of almost unearthly charm. The amazing lighting was concentrated entirely on this loch and its surrounding lofty hills. Elsewhere in every direction the vision was one of unrelieved gloom. A few moments later the lighting ceased, just as if switched off by some unseen power. This strange and beautiful scene I have never forgotten.

CHAPTER SEVENTEEN

KINLOCHBERVIE TO CAPE WRATH

ROM the door of Sandwood Cottage it is just possible to see the Cape Wrath lighthouse, but this can equally well be seen by climbing the highest hill near Sheigra. So I took to the road again, and drove towards a region of desolate moorland, strewn here and there with great boulders deposited by melting glaciers of the Ice Age. The sandy track kept some distance inland, giving frequent glimpses of the sea. This district is very sparsely populated, but it was not always so. The neighbourhood of Oldshore was once well-wooded, cultivated, and quite populous. At Oldshore Beg nearby, King Haco of Norway is said to have landed in the thirteenth century.

The road is quite feasible for motoring, and the mail bus goes as far as Balchreick and Sheigra, passing the footpath leading down to Droman and the lovely rocky cove at Port Chaligaig. I came to one or two gates which were opened by rosy-faced frolicsome children, who smiled at me delightedly. Much gratified at this warm reception I distributed coins and a few old newspapers, which pleased them greatly. I bumped along towards Sheigra; the children ran behind, and had caught up by the time the next gate was reached.

The road terminated at Sheigra Cottages, where the little boys and girls danced around, the local population turned out, and a venerable patriarch with a long white beard beamed upon me with placid interest. I asked him if it was possible to drive any further towards Cape Wrath. As the road ended at a cottage and the maps showed no road of any kind beyond this point, I felt that my question was hardly necessary. Hence my surprise when the old gentleman courteously indicated a footpath stretching northwards over a desolate expanse of moorland, and said that I could drive a little further towards Sandwood Loch. He then opened a narrow gate beside the cottage and waved me through. I just squeezed the car through the gateway, bounced along to the edge of a stream and lurched across.

A track of sorts led onwards, climbing to the shoulder of Cnoc Poll a Mhurain, the biggest hill in the neighbourhood. Leaving the long-suffering car I climbed over the boulder-strewn slopes to the summit, from where I had a wonderful view.

I felt as if I were the only man on earth. Visibility was tremendous, but there was no sign of human habitation anywhere. In time I was able to sort out the various landmarks, and despite the crystal clarity of the day, my amazement grew. All our old friends were there and looking their best. The Point of Stoer, twenty miles away, was the most prominent feature of the coastline, although the 400-foot red sandstone cliffs of Handa, ten miles distant, looked quite near and very distinctive. The Coigach mountains (over forty miles distant) and Suilven (thirty miles away) were clearly visible. Almost every Sutherland mountain competed to enhance this view. Quinag, Glas Bheinn, Ben More Assynt, Conaveall, Ben Stack, Ben Arkle, Foinaven and Cranstackie formed a mighty chain of overwhelming grandeur.

I looked to the west across the Atlantic to the distant line of the Outer Hebrides seen from the Butt of Lewis to the mountains of Harris, over fifty miles away. But I found my greatest thrill in looking north across Strath Shinary to the Moors of the Parph, and seeing Cape Wrath and the light-house gleaming white in the morning sunlight.

I have always regarded Cape Wrath as the Ultima Thule of Scotland. It is infinitely harder to reach than the much more frequently visited John o' Groats. On a perfect day this is a region of clear blue skies, white billowy clouds, golden sands, stupendous pink cliffs, luscious brown moorland and lonely lochans, with gentle summer zephyrs stirring their quiet waters into a myriad of tiny ripples. The great cliffs stretching towards Sandwood Bay and Cape Wrath are the haunts of gulls, cormorants, guillemots and razor-bills. The scene is enchanting in ideal weather, but it is a terrible place in storm and tempest.

I looked towards the coast, and was surprised to see what appeared to be the jawbones of a prehistoric monster. On closer inspection this turned out to be a curious rock formation at the extreme edge of the cliffs a mile away. This strange sight aroused my curiosity, so I set forth on a hurried scramble round tiny lochans, across swamps and streams and over outcrops of rock.

My objective was frequently out of sight as I dipped down into hollows and crossed peat bogs. At length I halted by the shores of a lochan, amazingly situated near the extreme edge of the cliffs.

A long, sinister tooth of rock projected above the cliff edge, and a solid squat stack of rock kept it company. A little to one side a sheer wall of cliff jutted still higher, giving a fearsome impression of the terrifying downward plunge of the entire line of cliffs. The intense silence was overpowering. There was a peculiar earthy smell as I stood on the dried banks of sun-baked mud, and the lone tooth of rock looked as if I had just interrupted it in conversation with the adjacent stack. It only remained for a pterodactyl to flap its leathery wings and flop down on to the rock to complete a picture that had in it all the elements of a first-class nightmare.

As I came away I gave a farewell glance towards Sandwood Bay, a delightful spot in fine weather, and in vivid contrast to the strange scene just described. There must always be a feeling of mystery about this remote district, a feeling that strange and curious things have happened and would happen again if you stayed long enough. Nothing stranger or more remarkable could possibly happen than the amazing encounter of Sandy Gunn, a local shepherd, with a mermaid on the 5th of January, 1900.

I had heard about this story from Donald McLeod, former proprietor of the Garbet Hotel, and it seemed worth investigating. It was not until July 1939, following a lengthy correspondence with Mr McLeod, that I was able to publish an account of the whole extraordinary incident in *Scotland's* (*SMT*) *Magazine*. Mr McLeod, armed with a batch of my most searching questions, interviewed the shepherd, whom he had known for many years, and thus obtained every detail of his meeting with the mermaid. It is from the shepherd's answers to my written questionnaire that I have been able to reconstruct the following strange and unusual account.

It was a calm clear afternoon, as the lone shepherd strode towards the coast in search of his flock. His faithful collie was close at heel, and when the sheep were found it seemed a pity to return to his lonely cottage, so he decided to descend to the golden sands of Sandwood Bay and take a quiet stroll. The great Atlantic rollers were surging across the smooth expansive sands, and apart from the occasional call of a gull and the sound of the surf, there was nothing to be heard. It was a very quiet evening, and there was a wistful charm and subtle ethereality characteristic of the neighbourhood. Sometimes on such occasions the veil is lifted and one is permitted to see some of the enchanting mysteries seldom revealed. It was good to feel the tang of the salt spray and watch the splendour of the setting sun on this lovely coast. The shepherd felt at peace with the world as he walked along the glistening sands.

As he approached a ledge of rock he saw that he was no longer alone. Something was reclining on the rock, but he could not quite see what it was. His dog seemed very uneasy, and kept close beside him. The shepherd crept to within twenty yards, and to his undisguised amazement saw that he was looking at a mermaid. She was very charming. Her figure, so far as it conformed to human standards, was almost perfect, and she had the loveliest golden curly hair and beautiful blue eyes. She had not long emerged from the sea, and was busy arranging her curls which lay in untidy profusion on her creamy skin. She was quite happy, and certainly did not expect any company, as she gave an occasional glance across lonely Sandwood Bay.

The shepherd was entranced yet afraid, because he had no idea what the mermaid would do. His collie was terrified, and he could expect little help there. Suddenly the mermaid saw him. Their eyes met, and in that moment the shepherd knew what it was to feel really scared. She seemed a little frightened at first, but continued to stare at the intruder a little resentfully. Her appearance was printed indelibly on the shepherd's mind during this amazing encounter, and he even noticed her rather short white hands and broad powerful fish-like tail. Fascinating though she was, the shepherd thought it better to retreat, which he did with great caution, the mermaid making no move, but steadily watching him as he made his careful exit.

In his *Wade the River, Drift the Loch*, R. Macdonald Robertson gives a photograph of Sandy Gunn, together with a translation from the Gaelic of his own account of the meeting with the mermaid.

I thought of this vivid account as I drove to Kinlochbervie on my most recent visit. It was a wild and tempestuous night, and the wind tore at the car as I crept along the road along the cliffs towards Achriesgill. The west wind had now attained gale force, and I fervently hoped that it would subside in time for me to complete my journey on the morrow. It was impossible to stand upright as I battled my way into the Garbet Hotel.

I made careful inquiry on the subject of approaching Cape Wrath, and was told of a new approach consisting of a peat track leading from Blairmore to Loch na Gainimh. It was considered possible to get a car to within about a quarter of a mile of Loch a' Mhuillinn, a mile and a half beyond the north-east corner of Loch na Gainimh. Next morning enthusiasm sank to vanishing point. The gale, so far from subsiding, was now a regular hurricane from the south-west. It was a shocking day, and I knew that beyond Loch na Gainimh I could expect nothing but a wilderness of bog and peat hags stretching to the grim Moors of the Parph. Only the knowledge that this was the climax to my tour gave me the necessary resolution to start on this mad expedition.

At Blairmore I looked for the track without much success, and finally inquired at a crofter's cottage. I was directed along a rough road and had to negotiate a couple of gates, a formidable feat in such a gale. After a steady climb my route degenerated into a peat-track paved with large boulders. Only a most intimate knowlege of the car's anatomy made it possible to crawl along, even in bottom gear. Frightful though it was to go on, it was impossible to turn back. At length I reached Loch na Gainimh, and negotiated the boulder-strewn track to the far end of the loch.

Here I encountered another peat track which I followed grimly and most unhappily. All hope vanished as the track disappeared into a peat bog, and I learned that there is such a word as impossible. It is just possible to turn a car here.

It was now necessary to part company with the car, and the more I looked at the wilderness ahead, the less I liked it. At first it seemed possible to discern the outline of a track, but this proved illusory. The nearby waters of the loch were lashed into vigorous waves with spray carrying in the wind, a most cheerless sight.

I had made all possible preparations, and wore every item of clothing I possessed. It required the utmost care to open the car door, otherwise it would have been torn off its hinges. Once outside I felt the icy blast of the wind, and struggled into a thick mackintosh worn over my coat. Thus

och Glencoul and
en Leoid from
napool

NORTH-WEST SUTHERLAND

ch Inchard,
inaven and Ben
kle from
nlochbervie

*Canisp and Suilv
from Torbreck*

NORTH-WEST SUTHERLAND

*Eddrachillis Bay
from Badcall*

attired, and with two camera outfits inside a large case strapped on my back, I plunged into the unknown.

From the track above Loch Clais na Coinneal the route lay downhill, with the gale almost behind. Sandwood Loch and Bay were not quite visible, but the gap where they were could be seen ahead. Beyond that the bleak swampy moors extended to the outline of Cape Wrath. The last remnants of the path soon vanished, but I thought that if I could get across the intervening couple of miles I should be in Strath Shinary, where there might be a track. Somehow the awful crossing was made, and I only fell into a swamp once, filling my shoes with peat-water. A passing cloudburst soon adjusted the balance, but far underneath my canopy of clothes I was still comparatively dry.

I came to Sandwood Loch, which must be beautiful indeed in fine weather, followed a sheep-track to the ruins of Sandwood Cottage, and continued to the green machair between the loch and the bay. I could now see the great line of cliffs, Cape Wrath itself, and even the lighthouse on the top. I then climbed seawards towards the top of the cliffs to the south of Sandwood Bay. It was an anxious business taking photographs in such an exposed position, with the wind trying to hurl me from the cliffs. I made a careful detour to descend to the bay, and finished by sliding down high sand drifts. There was an unpleasant sand-storm in progress, which soon filled my shoes.

The tide was at low ebb, and far across the bay great foam-flecked waves were attacking a pile of rocks. The hurricane blew the spindrift in a continuous stream of spray. The tide was evidently on the turn as I fought my way across the sands, scrambled on to the seaweed-strewn rocks, and took a quick look northwards towards the range of immense cliffs leading to Cape Wrath. A further glance southwards revealed more enormous cliffs, and a solitary isolated pinnacle known as the 'Herdsman'.

There was little time to see more, as wicked swirling tongues of water, the vanguard of tremendous waves, were trying to surround the rocks on which I was standing. No doubt I was on the very rocks where the mermaids were apt to sun-bathe, but mermaids are sensible creatures and do not venture foolishly into the teeth of hurricanes.

With great difficulty I took one or two photographs, and looked back from where I had come—back into the raging sand-storm and across to the gap in the cliffs and the horrors beyond. This was the climax of my tour, and Cape Wrath lay in full view. The vicious spume-covered waves were now isolating the rocks on which I stood, and I was becoming saturated by the spindrift.

I could not face the sand-storm, so had to retreat backwards, covering quite a lot of Sandwood Bay before I reached the sand-dunes. During my progress I noticed—so far as I could notice anything—many remnants of wrecks. It was far from easy climbing the fifteen-foot sand dunes in the teeth of the gale, and time and time again I was flung back. Dark storm clouds were blowing up, and my position was becoming serious. At length I reached the top, and made a supreme effort to reach Sandwood Cottage before the deluge.

When inhabited this must have been the loneliest cottage on the mainland of Scotland. Now that it was deserted and ruined it seemed the most desolate spot on earth. But once inside I had the eerie sensation of being watched. I felt as a strange insect might feel on the slide of a microscope! I could find nothing among the wreckage of the interior to offer a clue to this unusual feeling. It is possible that imagination plays strange tricks when one is tired to the point of exhaustion, but I must admit to preferring the known horrors of the inferno outside to the unseen mysteries of the interior.

My return to the car was real enough. I fought the gale for three hours, but the downpour had passed, and only the gale remained. Occasional fitful sunlight gave slight encouragement. It was impossible to hold my compass steady, so I kept near the coast, worked my way southwards, and climbed the slopes of Cnoc Poll, hoping to see the car. The outlook was very different from that entrancing scene on that lazy September day when I had last climbed this hill. Now I was like a drowning man clutching at a straw.

But my hopes were not in vain. Far across the desolate expanse of moor a tiny speck of light danced like a will o' the wisp. It was the sun flashing on the car windscreen. There was still a long way to go, and my encounter with another bog delayed my progress. But I could now see the car, and made the effort of a lifetime to get there, unlock the door and climb inside. All told, I had fought the hurricane for over six hours, and the sand-storm at Sandwood Bay had not improved matters.

My great fear was that the engine would not start. However, it did so at the first touch, and I was able to drive very slowly over the execrable track to Blairmore and continue to Kinlochbervie. After my grim battle with the elements, the Garbet Hotel seemed like a green oasis in an interminable desert.

The wild weather continued as I returned to Rhiconich and followed the lonely road to Keoldale, near Durness. This is now a first-class motoring road, and a continuation of the Lairg-Laxford Bridge route. The long but gradual climb up the Achriesgill valley gave many views across to Foinaven and the tangle of lochs on Gualin Moor. I passed Gualin House, once a place of refuge and now a shooting lodge, and then descended Strath Dionard towards the Kyle of Durness. The river is crossed at Drochaid Mhor, about four miles from the far side of the Keoldale Ferry. If only a passable road were made to connect these two points it would be possible to drive all the way to Cape Wrath, and it is not unreasonable to assume that such a route would attract many tourists who could not otherwise reach this majestic north-western tip of Scotland.

The Kyle of Durness was a magnificent sight as I drove steadily northwards to Keoldale. The gale had still not blown itself out, and the storm-tossed clouds above the glistening sands of the Kyle made an unforgettable picture against the grim background of the hills of Fashven, Scrishven and the Moors of the Parph.

The only feasible tourist approach to Cape Wrath is from Keoldale. I can fairly claim to have exhausted the possibilities of approach from Sheigra to Sandwood Bay. Although I had obtained many impressive views of both Cape Wrath and the lighthouse from the rocks of Sandwood Bay, I had still been separated by six miles of trackless wastes, unbridged rivers and streams, hopeless stretches of swamp and the awful desolation of the Moors of the Parph. Sandwood Bay may be considered the nearest feasible tourist approach from the south, and even under ideal conditions it is not an easy walk. My own attempt in atrocious weather may give some idea of the conditions one is likely to meet.

The position is very different if the approach is made from Keoldale. Once across the ferry there is a road all the way to Cape Wrath lighthouse. But cars cannot be ferried across, and the road is now in a very bad state of repair, with a difficult ford between Achmor and Dail. So far as I know, the only vehicle which now crosses this eleven mile route over the Moors of the Parph is a lorry which occasionally travels from the Cape Wrath lighthouse to the ferry to pick up provisions. It may thus be possible to obtain a lift one way only. Perhaps the easiest method of all would be by motor cycle, which could be taken across the ferry.

I had some hopes of obtaining a lift to the lighthouse and walking back to the ferry, but the wild weather continued longer than I could stay. In fine weather, however, this walk over the loneliest and most inaccessible road on the mainland of Britain should be well worth while. The local postman manages to accomplish it three times a week by cycle, but the road is so bad that it should not take much longer to walk.

Cape Wrath itself is a magnificent sight. I have sailed round it several times in the battleship *Rodney*, and seen it under varying conditions. I remember it best on a fine sunny evening. The cliffs of the Cape range from 370 to 523 feet in height, and consist of grey gneiss with rich veins of pink pegmatite. On this glorious evening the cliffs gleamed with a delicate reddish colour, making a scene of great beauty. The cliffs increase in height towards the south-east of the headland, where they appear to be composed of red Torridonian sandstone.

Cape Wrath is the furthest limit of Scotland's western seaboard, and if you should arrive on a clear day and climb to the lighthouse balcony you will be able to see North Rona, the Butt of Lewis, the mountains of Harris, the Stack Rock and the Orkneys. But the view I shall be most interested to see will cover the short distance to Sandwood Bay and the rocks upon which I stood on that dreadful day of hurricane and tempest when it seemed I must surely be stormbound.

of Durness,
dale and the
s of the
h : hurricane,

NORTH-WEST SUTHERLAND

inag from
lestrome

Quinag from Loch Nedd

NORTH-WEST SUTHERLAND

Cape Wrath the rocks far sea from San Bay at ebb Note the hun blowing the of the waves wards

84

Here, at Cape Wrath, we must bid farewell to the western seaboard. We have followed this adventurous coastline through all the ramifications of its amazing contours, and we have also seen something of the adjacent islands from Ailsa Craig to the Hebrides. Loch by loch, headland by headland and mountain by mountain our journey has worked up to its climax at Cape Wrath. Now that our journey is ended we can return to the south as speedily as our northbound progress was leisurely. The route from Durness to Lairg and Inverness is but the preliminary to the fast Great North Road to Perth, Edinburgh and England. As we hasten southwards let us look forward to another visit to Cape Wrath, perhaps next time by way of the eastern and northern seaboards. But that is the story of another journey and an adventure for another book.

As I headed southwards through this kindly land I had a host of memories for company. They were, on the whole, very pleasant company.

There were memories of great beauty and some of exquisite fragrance—the Pass of the Cattle at sunset, Loch Buie in Mull, early morning at Portsonachan, Eddrachillis Bay coloured by the westering sun, the magic of Staffa and the peace of Iona; memories of majesty and splendour—Glencoe, Glen Shiel, Mam Rattachan, the Cuillin of Skye and Suilven; memories of sheer pleasure—a golden evening aboard the *King George V* gliding down the Sound of Mull, the drive round Arran and the yacht trip down Loch Etive; memories of excitement and awe—the relentless force of the flooded Nith at Dumfries, the lure of Corrievreckan, the horrors of Corriehalloch, Coruisk in rain and wind, the hurricane on my wild scramble towards Cape Wrath, the haunted cottage at Sandwood and the elusive mermaids on the beach, Loch Ness and its monster, the solitude of Quinag summit, the lonely roads of Morvern and Moidart and the grandeur of Loch Glencoul; and, lastly, there were memories of the past—the Road to the Isles, Prince Charlie, Montrose and Dr Johnson; Glencoe, Appin, Dunvegan and Duart; and, peering deep into the mists of time, the dauntless courage of the Saints— Ninian, Columcille, Maelrubha, Brendan, Kenneth and Moluag—bringing the teaching of Christ to the tangle of the Isles.

With but half such memories as these a man would find it in his heart to come back again and again to this favoured land.

PHOTOGRAPHIC NOTES

THE western seaboard of Scotland offers outstanding scope for pictorial photography; it is literally a photographer's paradise. The sublime beauty of the Western Highlands is at once a challenge and an inspiration. It may fairly be said that no other part of Britain can compare with this colourful coast, and I doubt whether such a combination of mountain, sea, and loch scenery could be surpassed anywhere else.

If any criticism can be found, it may be on the ground that the western seaboard—from the Mull of Kintyre to Cape Wrath—possesses a certain similarity. To those unfamiliar with the terrain, and to whom names of mountains, villages and lochs do not come as old friends, presentation of a large number of pictorially beautiful but somewhat similar scenes may pall. To offset this possible disadvantage it has been my aim to present as great a variety of scenes and atmospheric conditions as circumstances would permit. To this end I have used my cameras from dawn to dusk in all kinds of weather, covering all types of scene.

The best months for photography are May and June, with September a bad third. Very variable weather can be expected in May in the far north-west, when violent snow and hailstorms, blizzards and tempests are far from rare. But these conditions soon disperse and give way to magnificent cloudscapes and a rich luminosity at times of transcending beauty. On such occasions the sheer brilliance of colour and clarity produce results almost beyond description to one who has never seen them.

To portray the bewildering variety of atmospheric conditions calls for much careful planning and study. The more versatile the camera equipment used the better the results are likely to be, so long as you can ring the necessary changes in technique. In this connexion although there is much to be said for the miniature—still more can be said for the larger camera of equal versatility. Every photographer must work out his own technique, and my own methods are set out in the tabulated data at the end of these notes. It has always been my practice to note down all relevant data at the time and on the spot, and the value of this habit has proved incalculable in my work.

In essence the problems are twofold—technical and artistic. Technique to the professional photographer or advanced amateur can become almost automatic, and only thus can one concentrate on the far greater problems of composition and atmosphere. Much has been written about the 'seeing eye', 'painting with light' and so on, but as I see it certain places possess their own luminosity—an elusive quality going beyond atmosphere and almost akin to personality—Fingal's Cave, the Bealach-na-Ba and Suilven are typical examples.

Turning to technique, the obvious starting point is to use first-class precision-made equipment, preferably giving a negative at least $3\frac{1}{4}'' \times 2\frac{1}{4}''$ and employing interchangeable lenses of varying focal length, interchangeable roll-holders to permit use of the most suitable film for the subject, a wide variety of colour filters to give emphasis and visual impact to the features they are intended to enhance, a photo-electric exposure meter as a basis for exposure calculation, and a suitable lens-hood. Tripods are not much use in a wind, but a unipod is always a help.

Panchromatic film is an absolute essential, and whether fast, medium or slow is a matter of choice for the subject on hand. Roughly speaking very fast films are slightly grainy when subjected to very considerable enlargement, but they give a rather soft rendering very useful at times; the converse applies in proportion to the decreasing speed of the film. It is surprising how few realise that a fast panchromatic film may be four times faster than a slow fine grain panchromatic emulsion. This great speed makes it possible to use a smaller stop and so increase the depth of focus, an important factor in landscape work.

In the Western Highlands the beauty is very often in the highlights. Many of my best photographs were obtained by deliberately reversing the old adage of exposing for the shadows and letting the highlights take care of themselves. My experience is that they do not take care of themselves. When over-exposed they clog up and the beauty is gone.

All my cloudscapes are genuine, and were part of the original scene and not added afterwards. To my mind faked photographs are a travesty; photomontage and truth are incompatible, and one cannot capture the beauty of the original by resorting to fake. This self evident fact may give rise to criticisms of 'mere record work'. Nevertheless one can always discriminate, and as I see it there *is* beauty in the world, and it is up to us to seek it out, portray it to the best of our ability and not try to improve on nature. One must, therefore, wait for the right moment, the right effect of light and shade, the right cloud formation, and then primarily expose for the highlights except in such cases where at least minimum shadow detail is essential to the picture. Such negatives are often difficult to print, but generally yield in the end to the right kind of projection control, and in no other way can one capture the rich luminosity and ethereality of west coast highlights. If I have any secrets this is one of them, and it is surprising how far one can go in this direction, Plate 26 being an outstanding example. The combination of a very slow fine grain film, a yellow filter tripling the required exposure, autumn lighting, a very fast shutter speed and a comparatively modest lens aperture—all these factors would seem to spell disaster in the shape of a blank film. Yet this experiment—and it *was* an experiment—resulted in successful capture of the essential atmosphere of the scene.

For many years I have been able to familiarise myself with the western seaboard, and thus visualise the best lighting and atmospheric effects for a wide variety of scenes. My problem lies in getting to the right scene at the right time. One example will suffice—Plate 69—Sunset from the Bealach-na-Ba. It took twenty years to get there at the right moment, but I shall never forget the thrill of ultimate success and the sheer sublimity of the scene—to my mind the most majestic view from any road in Britain.

Finally, do not be afraid of impossibilities. Sometimes the impossible succeeds, and then the results, not being expected, are bound to exceed expectations. Occasionally they produce results which go much further and become hall-marks in a photographer's lifetime. Thus I am glad to have captured the innermost secrets of Fingal's Cave, the outline (however faint) of the Whirlpool of Corrievreckan, the back-wash of the tide-race at Staffa, the hurricane-lashed spindrift seen from the rocks of Sandwood Bay, and the golden splendour of the flooded Nith at Dumfries. Scenes like this may not be technical blue-prints, but they do possess atmosphere.

The raison d'etre for this book is, in the words of Keats, 'Beauty is truth, truth beauty'—and beauty is the essence of Scotland's western seaboard, a beauty I have tried to portray truthfully.

G. DOUGLAS BOLTON

PHOTOGRAPHIC DATA

Cameras	Lenses	Filters	Film
B = Kodak Bantam Special	E = F/2·0 Ektar (4·5 cm)	WY2 = Wratten Pale Yellow × 2	PX = Kodak Panatomic X
M = Plaubel Makina IIS (converted Makina III)	A = 10 cm F/2·9 Anticomar	PY2 = Plaubel Pale Yellow × 2	SX = Kodak Super XX
	O = 7·3 cm F/6·8 Wide Angle Orthar	PY3 = Plaubel Medium Yellow × 3	SH = Selo HP3
	T = 19 cm F/4·8 Tele-Makinar	PG4 = Plaubel Green × 4	PLX = Kodak Plus X
	AC, OC and TC indicate use of the relevant lens after coating; A, O and T refer to use before coating.	VY3 = Voigtlander Medium Yellow × 3	SF = Selo FP3
		RY2 = Rollei Pale Yellow × 2	GM = Gevaert Microgran
R = Rolleicord II	Z = 7·5 cm F/3·5 Zeiss Triotar		
V = Voigtlander Rangefinder Bessa	H = 10·5 cm. F/3·5 Heliar		

PHOTOGRAPHIC DATA (continued)

(N.B. A lens hood was used in all cases)

No. of Plate	Camera	Lens	Exposure	Stop	Filter	Film	Date
Outer Cover	M	T	1/100	6·3	PY3	SX	June 1
Frontispiece	M	OC	1/100	8·0	PY3	PLX	July 5
2.	M	T	1/25	6·3	PY2	SX	May 13
3.	M	O	1/100	6·8	PG4	PX	Sept. 7
4.	M	O	1/100	6·8	PG4	PX	Sept. 5
5.	M	O	1/100	6·8	PG4	PX	Sept. 5
6.	M	O	1/50	9·0	PY3	SX	May 12
7.	M	O	1/50	6·8	None	SH	Sept. 2
8.	M	O	1/50	6·8	PG4	PX	Sept. 2
9.	M	A	1/100	12·0	PY2	SX	June 26
10.	M	O	1/50	6·8	PG4	PX	Sept. 2
11.	M	A	1/100	11·0	PY3	SX	June 2
12.	M	A	1/100	6·0	PY3	SX	June 2
13.	B	E	1/100	4·0	None	PX	Aug. 23
14.	M	OC	1/25	9·0	PY3	SF	July 1
15.	M	OC	1/200	8·0	PY3	SH	June 30
16.	B	E	1/250	5·6	None	PX	Aug. 23
17.	M	A	1/50	7·0	PY3	SX	May 16
18.	M	A	1/50	7·0	PY3	SX	May 16
19.	M	A	1/100	9·0	PY3	SX	June 2
20.	M	A	1/100	6·0	PY3	SX	June 2
21.	M	A	1/50	10·0	PY3	SX	May 16
22.	M	T	1/50	7·0	PY3	SX	May 16
23.	M	AC	1/50	9·0	PY3	PLX	June 29
24.	M	TC	1/200	6·3	PY3	PLX	July 1
25.	M	OC	1/100	9·0	PY3	PLX	June 29
26.	V	H	1/400	5·6	VY3	GM	Sept. 24
27.	M	O	1/100	7·0	PY2	PX	Sept. 24
28.	M	OC	1/25	7·0	PY3	PLX	July 2
29.	M	O	1/50	6·8	PY2	PX	Sept. 24
30.	M	A	1/50	9·0	PY3	PX	Sept. 24
31.	M	O	1/50	8·0	PY2	PX	Sept. 24
32.	M	T	1/50	12·0	PY3	SX	May 20
33.	M	O	1/50	6·8	PY2	SX	June 1
34.	M	T	1/100	6·3	PY3	PX	Sept. 24
35.	M	TC	1/200	5·0	PY3	PLX	July 1
36.	M	A	1/50	6·0	None	SX	May 19
37.	V	H	1/50	5·6	VY3	SX	May 20
38.	M	T	1/100	6·3	PY3	SX	June 1
39.	M	OC	1/100	9·0	PY3	PLX	June 29
40.	M	OC	1/50	9·0	PY3	PLX	July 3
41.	M	OC	1/50	11·0	PY3	PLX	July 3

No. of Plate	Camera	Lens	Exposure	Stop	Filter	Film	Date
42.	M	OC	1/100	8·0	PY3	SH	July 4
43.	M	OC	1/100	8·0	PY3	SH	July 5
44.	M	OC	1/50	6·8	PY3	PLX	July 5
45.	M	OC	1/10	6·8	None	SH	July 5
46.	M	OC	1/100	9·0	PY3	PLX	July 4
47.	M	OC	1/50	9·0	PY3	PLX	July 4
48.	M	OC	1/50	9·0	PY3	PLX	July 5
49.	M	OC	1/10	6·8	None	SH	July 5
50.	R	Z	1/50	4·5	RY2	PX	July 27
51.	M	O	1/25	7·0	PY2	PX	Sept. 23
52.	V	H	1/50	8·0	VY3	SX	May 21
53.	M	A	1/100	7·0	PY3	SX	May 21
54.	M	T	1/100	9·0	PY3	SX	May 21
55.	M	O	1/50	11·0	PY2	PX	Sept. 23
56.	M	A	1/100	11·0	PY3	SX	May 21
57.	M	A	1/100	6·0	PY3	SX	May 22
58.	M	A	1/100	6·0	PY3	SX	May 22
59.	B	E	1/50	5·0	WY2	PX	May 22
60.	M	A	1/100	6·0	PY3	SX	May 24
61.	M	A	1/100	6·0	PY3	SX	May 24
62.	M	A	1/100	8·0	PY3	SX	May 24
63.	M	A	1/25	7·0	PY3	SX	May 21
64.	M	A	1/100	6·0	PY3	SX	May 24
65.	M	A	1/50	6·0	PY3	SX	May 22
66.	M	A	1/100	6·0	PY3	SX	May 23
67.	M	T	1/50	6·0	PY3	SX	May 20
68.	M	O	1/100	7·0	PY2	PX	Sept. 23
69.	M	A	1/50	5·6	PY3	SX	May 25
70.	M	A	1/100	6·0	PY3	SX	May 26
71.	M	A	1/100	6·0	PY3	SX	May 26
72.	M	A	1/100	6·0	PY3	SX	May 26
73.	V	H	1/50	5·0	VY3	PX	May 26
74.	M	A	1/100	6·0	PY3	SX	May 26
75.	M	A	1/100	4·5	PY3	SX	May 26
76.	V	H	1/100	8·0	VY3	SX	May 27
77.	M	A	1/50	4·5	PY3	SX	May 27
78.	M	O	1/100	9·0	PY3	SX	May 28
79.	M	T	1/100	6·3	PY3	SX	May 27
80.	M	A	1/100	4·5	PY3	SX	May 27
81.	M	O	1/100	6·8	PY3	SX	May 28
82.	M	A	1/50	9·0	PY3	SX	May 27
83.	M	A	1/100	6·0	PY3	SX	May 27
84.	M	A	1/200	6·0	PY3	SX	May 28

INDEX

N.B.—Bold figures refer to plates

INDEX

MAPS; 3, 47, 111.